Thoroughbred
Investor's
Bible

all the best –

Thoroughbred Investor's Bible

By John Perrotta

Edited by Jay Hovdey

Foreword by James L. Gagliano

Short Dog Publishing

Bulk orders of this book are available from the publisher at: www.shortdogpublishing.com

ISBN 978-0-578-31689-5

THOROUGHBRED INVESTOR'S BIBLE

TABLE OF CONTENTS

*This book is dedicated to all the hard-working and
honest racetrackers who labor so tirelessly
at the game they love, despite the endless hours and lack
of recognition, simply to be near the
horses we hold so dear.*

FOREWORD

The Jockey Club celebrated its 125th anniversary in 2019, and this occasion proved to be an opportunity for me to reflect, not just on The Jockey Club's evolution over the years, but also the industry itself. From electronic starting gates and digital foal certificates to advance-deposit wagering and the creation of the Breeders' Cup, Thoroughbred racing and breeding have experienced countless changes.

The industry's resilience was further tested by the effects of the COVID-19 pandemic, which turned the world upside down in March 2020 and continued to affect all aspects of our lives. Given evolving trends in the business attitudes toward animal welfare, and the lingering effects of the pandemic, I expect more developments than ever in the coming years.

It is no secret that animal welfare has become a significant priority in the eyes of the public, and these views have put increased pressure on all animal entertainment industries to enact meaningful reforms on behalf of animals or suffer the financial consequences. Horse racing has not been immune to this scrutiny and is facing greater accountability for the welfare of racehorses. Tracks across the country have implemented advanced screening and veterinary protocols to try to prevent potentially unsound horses from competing.

The Jockey Club has advocated for and supported a host of reforms to improve equine safety, including the Horseracing Integrity and Safety Act (HISA). This legislation, which was signed into law at the end of 2020, will establish national, uniform safety standards that include anti-doping and medication control and racetrack safety programs managed by an independent, self-regulatory authority. I look forward to seeing HISA take effect and witnessing the positive impacts that it will have on our industry.

In addition to oversight of active racehorses, the Thoroughbred industry has also seen heartening progress in recent years toward prioritizing aftercare for horses once their racing careers end. Initiatives such as the Thoroughbred Aftercare Alliance and Thoroughbred Incentive Program, both supported by The Jockey Club, continue to grow each year, promoting top standards in aftercare facilities as well as the versatility of Thoroughbreds to be used in other disciplines upon retirement from racing.

Another change we have seen in the sport is a different look to the top owners and trainers. While Thoroughbred ownership was once primarily composed of families and single entities, large syndicates made up of dozens, if not hundreds, of individuals now compete and succeed at the highest levels of our sport. One need only look at the vast ownership group of Justify, the 2018 Triple Crown winner, to see the potential of these syndicates. At the same time, racing clubs operated by racetracks and state associations offer minute stakes in horses to hundreds, increasing accessibility to Thoroughbred ownership.

The highest levels of racing are also now dominated by individuals deemed "super trainers." It is commonplace for top trainers to manage hundreds of horses spanning multiple states and racetracks. The long-term effects of this shift from smaller training operations remain to be seen.

In *Thoroughbred Investor's Bible*, my longtime friend John Perrotta has called on his diverse experiences in racing to provide potential owners and breeders with invaluable information to increase their chances of being successful in the sport of kings today, while keeping in mind the industry's current climate.

From his time on the backstretch and managing a racing and breeding operation to creating the Thoroughbred Racing Radio Network and involvement in the production of HBO's racing series *Luck*, John is well-versed in the intricacies of the industry. While sharing his plethora of knowledge, he also includes insights from other industry experts to solidify the comprehensiveness of this "bible." The book delves into all aspects of the industry from the basic racing rules to a roadmap for establishing an aftercare plan. No matter one's level of involvement or experience in the industry, the reader is sure to find the chapters enlightening.

Times have changed since John was walking hots and I was working in Monmouth Park's mailroom. The Thoroughbred industry faces a turbulent future, and stakeholders must be prepared to react to the changes and challenges thrown our way should we wish to be sustainable. John's work here offers tools for investors to be prepared for a changing landscape, one that the founders of The Jockey Club surely could not have foreseen when the organization was incorporated more than 125 years ago.

James L. Gagliano
President and Chief Operating Officer
The Jockey Club

PREFACE

My nearly 50 years of experience in racing has taken many twists and turns, and along the way I have observed thousands of successes and many more failures. I have tried to learn from my own mistakes and those of others, and I hope that those who read these pages will find something to help make their journey more successful, less costly, and every bit as joyous as mine has been.

I grew up in the horse country of rural New Jersey and attended a high school that was a Thoroughbred training center before its conversion to a place of education. I harvested hay from the fields of Colts Neck, walked hots and groomed horses, and worked as a racetrack usher, wiping off reserved seats for quarter tips at Monmouth Park during summers off from school. Upon finishing college, I had hopes of a career as a sportswriter, but soon I gravitated back to the racetrack and found myself a fledgling jockey's agent, an occupation I would stick with for over a decade.

In the summer of 1981, on the first day of the month of June, I took on a new venture of sorts: a management position in the racing business.

But that new venture, as executive director of financier Robert Brennan's recently formed Due Process Stable, would prove my true vocation. Over the following fifteen years I became the vice president and general manager of Brennan's racing and breeding operation, oversaw the building of farms in New Jersey, Florida, and Kentucky, and directed a skilled and enthusiastic staff of more than 200 employees.

The organization was motivated further by Brennan's acronym SCHRIDE, which stood for "Self-confidence, Courage, Honesty, Responsibility, Impatience with oneself - not others,

Determination, and Enthusiasm." I posted that motivator in barns, breeding sheds, and racehorse stables, and attired the entire crew with green tee-shirts echoing the sentiments.

Early on with Due Process, barely having dampened my feet, I was summoned to accompany my boss and our trainer, Reynaldo Nobles, on a trip to the Keeneland Summer Yearling Sale in Lexington, Ky. Nothing in my previous racetrack life had prepared me for what I was to witness in bluegrass country. When I signed on, we had 24 racehorses in our inventory. Within six months, I was overseeing a hundred, within two years, three hundred horses and three farms under the Due Process banner. I graduated from college with a bachelor's degree in philosophy, but I got my PhD at the racetrack, learning more from hustlers, grifters, and equine gamesmen than I ever could inside ivy covered walls.

It is from those unique characters that much of the wisdom shared in these pages was drawn, so please consider that most of the mistakes that you could make in the Thoroughbred business can be avoided by following the advice herein.

The aspirations of the potential Thoroughbred investor range from the career-driven Wall Street player who has amassed a fortune and now seeks a new outlet for his energy, to the three partners who have enjoyed success with their local business and have earned the right to rub elbows with the elite. All of them are looking for fun – and maybe even profit – and I hope the following chapters help steer toward that destination.

Have no delusions, though. Investing in Thoroughbreds is a significant business journey, travelled on a path fraught with unpredictable perils for those who don't take it seriously. Individuals who dabble or treat it lightly will find they've chosen an expensive hobby, something the tax boys will soon point out. Simply put, it's a path not meant for everyone.

As a person who has either witnessed or personally committed every mistake possible in the Thoroughbred game, I promise to offer as much insight into investing as can be found anywhere, and I will pull no punches in the process. Much of the advice will be presented as sets of rules to follow on the investing path, for, as any skilled poker player will tell you, the way to winning is to begin with a good starting hand.

So, for those intent on going forward, the contents of this book should be consumed as an operating manual. Follow the tenets put forth and you'll have, as the song goes, "The chance of a lifetime in a lifetime of chance."

-- J.P.

Thoroughbred Investor's Bible

Triple Crown winner Secretariat set a high bar.

CHAPTER 1

THE GREATEST GAME PLAYED OUTDOORS

"All men are equal on the turf – and under it."
~ Lord George Bentinck

Part of the allure of the racetrack is its romantic nature. Even today, well into the 21st century, the track is a throwback to an era populated by the colorful hustlers and gamblers of Damon Runyon's *Guys and Dolls* – wise guys and flashy dames with names like Sky Masterson, Miss Adelaide, and Nathan Detroit:

I got the horse right here, the name is Paul Revere,
And here's a guy that says if the weather's clear,
Can do. Can do. The guy says the horse can do.

In those days, going to the races and playing the ponies was as habitual as church on Sunday. The sport of horse racing ushered more fans through its turnstiles than baseball, football and basketball combined, or at least it did until the introduction of state lotteries became widespread in the 1970s, accompanied by the burgeoning popularity of golf and tennis through their explosion of coverage on television. The pages of the *Morning Telegraph* and the *Daily Racing Form* touted their coverage as "the world's authority on horse racing and boxing," and for good measure they included reviews on Broadway plays, just like the *New York Times*.

It would be cheery to think that horse racing's popularity could have been attributed to the love and appreciation of the magnificent animals, or perhaps to the chance of rubbing elbows with such Hollywood stars as Bing Crosby, Pat O'Brien, Bob Hope, Mickey Rooney, Jimmy Cagney, Lucille Ball, Betty Grable, and Rita Hayworth. They all were known to frequent the track, along with high-powered financiers, industrialists, and politicians, none of whom were shy of the press spotlight.

More likely, the answer to racing's popularity could be found in a simple fact: Racetracks were the only place the general population could place a legal wager.

The business of the game has changed dramatically since the 1970s, when horse racing lost its monopoly on legal gambling in the U.S. And yet, it still takes only one trip to the races for the unsuspecting fan to get hooked on the adrenaline rush of a winning bet, no matter what the odds.

Of all the sports that lend themselves to passionate commitment, Thoroughbred racing seems to be unique. Riddled with variables, dramatic to a fault, its daunting quest for the ultimate victory is infectious, evolving relentlessly from curiosity to fascination to obsession.

Business leaders, having enjoyed some measure of success in their chosen fields, look for a source of enjoyment and excitement in the world of sport as an outlet for relaxation, or as hobbyists. Owning a football, baseball, basketball, or hockey team would put them at the top of those heady worlds. Their burning desire to compete would be satisfied through identification with the team as a vicarious extension of their own egos.

But even the wealthiest entrepreneur might find it a stretch to come up with the half-a-billion to a billion dollars a professional team could cost. By comparison, a Thoroughbred racing stable can be established for a fraction of that investment. Suddenly, you are playing at the professional level with your own franchise for an amount that does not stick in the throat, accompanied by all the perks of ownership, including interviews on television. As the owner of a racing stable once told me:

"I could buy a yacht or a Picasso or a garage full of sports cars, but you can't feed a carrot to your boat or your painting or your car. And besides, I get to bring all my friends to the winner's circle to have their picture taken and share the fun when my horse wins."

Racehorses come in all shapes and sizes, and the sorting process to find talented equine athletes is no small challenge. Some start humbly, perhaps reflecting their purchase price or breeding, but even they can work their way up the class ladder to become that precious creature competing at the top of the game – the Thoroughbred known as the "Saturday horse" – racing at the greatest racetracks in the land.

There are the boutique racing meets at Keeneland in Kentucky, Del Mar in California, and Saratoga in upstate New York, where the elite of the sport mingle, and everyday fans flaunt the latest fashions. There are the high visibility events like the Triple Crown series, the Breeders' Cup, the Pegasus World Cup at Gulfstream, and Travers at Saratoga, not to mention international attractions like England's Royal Ascot, France's Arc de Triomphe, Australia's Melbourne Cup, the Japan Cup, and the Dubai World Cup. All of these serve to highlight the best of the sport's equine and human athletes while catching the attention of the general populace, if only because of the pretty people and noble Thoroughbreds.

If success in such events was only a matter of spending the most money, those races always would be won by the richest of the rich. But that ain't necessarily so because, quite literally, a good horse can come from almost anywhere.

Breeders of Thoroughbreds have many methods by which they endeavor to come up with a champion. By mating their own mares to an appropriate stallion, they adhere to the old adage of trying to "breed the best to the best and hope for the best." They also can enter into alliances and partnerships, some of which are referred to as "foal sharings," wherein one party provides the mare and the other provides the stallion, after which they either share or alternate ownership of the resulting foals.

The origins of an historic foal sharing took place one evening in 1968 when two of America's wealthiest families entered into an agreement that changed the face of modern racing.

Gladys Mills Phipps was the wife of Henry Carnegie Phipps, heir to a steel fortune and founder of Bessemer Trust. Together they established the Wheatley Stable of outstanding Thoroughbreds that included champion stallion Bold Ruler. Christopher Chenery acquired his fortune in oil, gas, and utilities while also making a name for his Meadow Stable horses that included champions Hill Prince and Cicada. The Phipps-Chenery foal sharing agreement would cover two years – the breeding seasons of 1968 and 1969 – during which time Chenery would send his prize mare Somethingroyal to Wheatley Stable's Bold Ruler.

A coin flip determined who would receive the first foal of Somethingroyal, and Phipps won the toss. That first foal was a filly, named The Bride, who lost her only four races and retired to accomplish little as a broodmare for the Wheatley brand. The second foal, however, was a different story. Chenery might have lost that coin toss, but in the end Meadow Stable won the lottery.

Named Secretariat, the handsome, powerful chestnut colt became a Triple Crown winner and two-time Horse of the Year, as the Meadow Stable's blue and white checked silks reigned as the most familiar colors in American racing. For the first time in history, a horse was a cover boy on major mainstream magazines like *Time*, *Newsweek*, and *Sports Illustrated*. Nearly a half century later, Secretariat was still rated No. 35 on ESPN's top 100 Athletes of the 20th century, above Mickey Mantle, Jack Dempsey, Bobby Jones, and Billie Jean King.

Clearly, in the case of Secretariat, breeding the best to the best worked like a charm. But that is an expensive path, and history tells us that sometimes lightning strikes in unpredictable ways.

Racing buddies Perry Martin and Steve Coburn were brought together through a Northern California racing syndicate that enjoyed a bit of success. They also failed to follow one of the first rules of Thoroughbred investment: Never fall in love with any horse.

Love the Chase, the horse in question, was already part of the syndicate when she was put up for sale at auction. As a racehorse she was not much, having won only one of her six starts in a contest that her trainer described as "the slowest maiden race all year." Martin and Coburn bought her anyway, for $8,000, with the plan of her becoming a broodmare. In 2010 she was bred to Lucky Pulpit, a stallion with a $2,500 stud fee whose mediocre career included only one stakes win in 22 starts and earnings slightly over $200,000. With expectations low for the resulting foal and their friends mocking them for their folly, Martin and Coburn decided to call their enterprise the DAP Stable, standing for Dumb Ass Partners.

Pushing back against fate, the partners indulged in dreams of glory. They looked at their flashy young colt with the glowing chestnut coat and four white stockings and imagined him running in nothing less than the Kentucky Derby. Gathering with their wives during a social evening at a Sacramento area tavern, they drew lots with suggested names for the colt from Coburn's well-worn Stetson and came up with

19

California Chrome was a one-in-a-million superstar.

"California Chrome," acknowledging not only the state of his birth but also his flashy white trim.

From dreams come hopes, and from hopes sometimes comes incredible success. The partners sent California Chrome to Southern California in the spring of 2013 to be trained by the 76-year-old veteran Art Sherman, a former jockey. Sherman thought the young colt could be a stakes winner of some kind, a prediction that came true at Del Mar that summer and then again at the end of the year when California Chrome won the King Glorious Stakes on the final day of racing at Hollywood Park.

The quick chestnut opened his three-year old year by winning the San Felipe Stakes and Santa Anita Derby. Suddenly, the Dumb Ass Partners had the favorite for the

Kentucky Derby. On the first Saturday in May 2014, California Chrome made the wild dreams of his owners come true, and in the bargain, he made Sherman the oldest trainer to ever win the Kentucky Derby – all from breeding far from the best to even farther from the best and hoping for a miracle.

Two weeks after the Derby, California Chrome galloped home a winner again in the Preakness Stakes to set up a chance at the elusive Triple Crown. But he could only finish in a dead-heat for fourth in the Belmont Stakes and emerged from the race with a nasty leg wound. He returned to the races later in the year and performed well enough to earn the title as three-year old champion and Horse of the Year.

California Chrome's four-year-old season was abbreviated by foreign travel and a minor injury, but the time off did him good. As a five-year-old he returned to top form, winning the Dubai World Cup and the Pacific Classic on his way to a second title as Horse of the Year. He went to stud in 2017 with career earnings of $14,752,650, a record at the time.

Not bad for a $10,500 investment.

Neither was the $17,500 spent at the 1975 Fasig-Tipton summer sale in Lexington for a gangly, dark bay yearling by Bold Reasoning. Named Seattle Slew by his Washington State owners, the colt thrilled racing fans when he became the first undefeated Triple Crown winner in 1977. By the end of his career, Seattle Slew had banked more than $1.2 million while earning championships for three consecutive seasons, including 1977 Horse of the Year. He was sold as a stallion for $300,000 per share in a 40-share syndicate, for a total valuation of a tidy $12 million, after which he became one of the world's leading sires whose stud fee rose to a giddy $800,000 per mare at its peak. This is pretty much the definition of turning a minor investment into owning a bank.

The payoffs on investments in Secretariat, California Chrome, and Seattle Slew came in relatively short order. A solid floor to their value was pretty firmly established once they won the Kentucky Derby. However, some Thoroughbreds take time to realize their full potential.

In 1976, a smallish, unfashionably bred yearling came off the Golden Chance Farm near Paris, Ky., and was deemed unsuitable by experts for his conformational fault of being "back at the knee," a particular flaw considered one of the most undesirable. So unattractive was the colt that he only managed to bring $1,100 at the Keeneland January sale of horses of all ages. His buyer, J. E. Colloway, decided after feeding the young horse for a year that he'd had enough and sold him at the same Keeneland sale the following January for $2,200. Obviously, no money was made on that transaction.

The next buyer, Hal Snowden, Jr., gave his bargain basement two-year-old some early lessons, removed his testicles, and sold him to a Japanese client, but he was returned to Snowden soon afterwards because of those troubling knees. By now named John Henry, after the steel-driving man of the American legend, the gelding managed to win a stakes race in Louisiana for still another owner before Snowden, an old-school horse trader, repurchased him in the spring of 1978.

Snowden sold John Henry again for $25,000, sight unseen, to the Dotsam Stable of New York bicycle salesman Sam Rubin and his wife, Dorothy. By now John Henry was getting the idea, and he was at least earning his keep with trainer Robert Donato. Eventually, Rubin switched John Henry to Victor "Lefty" Nickerson, one of the top trainers in New York, who then recommended the owner send his one-horse stable to California, where he would benefit from the firm grass courses of Santa Anita and Hollywood Park. Ron McAnally, Nickerson's close friend, took over the training.

The rest became horse racing history. Under McAnally's care, John Henry went on to win 25 stakes races – including the inaugural Arlington Million and two runnings of the Santa

Anita Handicap – for total earnings of nearly $6.6 million. Before he was retired at age 10, John Henry would win seven Eclipse Awards, two of them for Horse of the Year honors in 1981 and 1984.

As a gelding, John Henry's procreative life was limited to longing glances at the opposite sex. Instead, as a pensioner, he became a popular attraction at the Kentucky Horse Park near Lexington and lived to a ripe old 32.

On and on, these fairy tales have come true:

In 1998, a homely three-year old colt called Real Quiet won the Derby and the Preakness and barely missed winning the Triple Crown when Victory Gallop beat him by a nose in the Belmont Stakes. Nicknamed "The Fish" around the barn for his narrow frame, Real Quiet blossomed into the champion three-year old of his generation, earning owner Mike Pegram more than $3.2 million before retiring at a $25,000 stud fee. His original price tag? -- $17,000.

In 1988, it would have taken only $17,000 to buy a 2-year-old by the name of Sunday Silence at a California sale. He failed to attract that reserve price, however, and ended up racing for his breeder and two partners. Sunday Silence not only won the 1989 Kentucky Derby and the Preakness, but he also later took the Breeders' Cup Classic and honors as Horse of the Year. Sunday Silence finished his career with $4.9 million in earnings before being sold to Zenya Yoshida for his Shadai Stallion Station on the island of Hokaido, where he became Japan's leading stallion for thirteen consecutive seasons, 1995 to 2008.

Proving that there is more than one way to catch that lightning, Florida breeder Rachel Carpenter bequeathed her horses upon her death to her longtime trainer, W.A. "Jimmy" Croll. Having trained Mr. Prospector, an outstanding racehorse who became a champion sire, Croll knew a good horse when he saw one. Carpenter's gift horse, named Holy Bull, was destined to put Croll in the Hall of Fame. During his 1994 Horse of the Year campaign, Holy Bull won the Florida Derby, the Blue Grass Stakes, the Met Mile, the Travers, and the Haskell Invitational for more than $2.4 million in earnings.

Then there was the tale of Hubert "Sonny" Hine, whose colorful career outside of racing included a stint in Hong Kong working for the CIA. When he came home to the U.S. and commenced a career as an owner, breeder, and trainer of Thoroughbreds, he piled up more than 1,300 wins and eventually landed a place in the Thoroughbred Racing Hall of Fame.

Hine's crowning achievement was the gray colt he picked out at the 1995 two-year-olds in training sale in Ocala, Fla., for $30,000. Hine's wife, Carolyn, named the colt Skip Away, and Hine, a true raconteur, enjoyed telling anyone who would listen how he chose the colt principally on his color. Supposedly, Carolyn's eyesight was failing, and Sonny wanted her to be able to find her horse in a crowded field. As it turned out, the view was wonderful. Skip Away earned $9.6 million, three divisional championships, and the title as 1998 Horse of the Year.

Of course, I would be remiss if I ignored the strikeouts, which number many more than the home runs. One of the most notable flops was a Northern Dancer colt out of the champion mare My Bupers who sold at the Keeneland summer yearling sale of 1983 for $10.2 million to Sheikh Mohammed bin Rashid al Maktoum of the United Arab Emirates. Later named Snaafi Dancer, the colt was such an embarrassment as a potential racehorse that he never started, and after proving to be sub-fertile, he was exiled to a farm in Florida where he lived out his days in obscurity.

In a folly even more expensive and nearly as embarrassing, the Irish Coolmore syndicate anteed up $13.1 million in 1985 for another son of Northern Dancer, christened Seattle Dancer.

He at least managed to win a minor stakes race in a brief career while earning a little more than $150,000 before he was sold for a song to a stud farm in Japan.

Total return on investment for the two Northern Dancer colts? How about minus $23 million. So much for the best to the best.

The common thread running through these tales is the unavoidable fact that luck plays a great hand in the game. But they also have another thing in common. The folks who enjoyed the good kind of luck put themselves in the right place at the right time, did their homework, and associated with the right people.

Those who follow the paths charted in these pages will have a much better chance to get run over by that good kind of luck.

Churchill Downs on Derby Day is racing's Holy Grail.

CHAPTER 2

RULES OF THE GAME

"You don't play this game in short pants."
~ Hall of Fame trainer LeRoy Jolley

LeRoy Jolley trained a host of champions and major stakes winners during his sixty-year career. He won the Kentucky Derby twice, including the 1980 running with Genuine Risk, one of only three fillies to win America's most famous horse race. Known to his contemporaries as an intelligent man with a quick and cutting wit, Jolley was never shy about expressing his opinion and never one to take any guff from one of his patrons.

"There are two kinds of trainers," Jolley would say. "The ones that got fired and the ones that are going to get fired."

Jolley's old saw about racing being anything but a kid's game is evergreen as well. The business is tough, challenging at all levels. Participation requires a maturity that can withstand serious setbacks, both financial and emotional. The rewards can be amazing, and there are people – and books like this – that can help the Thoroughbred investor enjoy those rewards with minimal frustration. But it is necessary to go into the sport with eyes wide open.

How tough is the game? Tough enough that it once needed the help of America's No. 1 lawman.

27

In the early 1940s, the powers of the sport asked FBI Director J. Edgar Hoover to form an organization intended to preserve the integrity of horse racing. Hoover was a racing aficionado – he was a regular at tracks near Washington, D.C. – and racing leaders were concerned that their enterprise would get caught up in the negative public opinion being heaped upon other sports due to incessant scandals and allegations of bribery and "fixed" games.

With Hoover's support, in 1946 the Thoroughbred Racing Protective Bureau was incorporated as a private investigative agency whose principal mission was to address issues of integrity and security in the Thoroughbred racing industry. Selected to head the organization was Spencer Drayton, Sr., a former FBI agent who for many years served as Hoover's administrative assistant. To a large extent, Drayton modeled the TRPB on the FBI and enlisted other former agents to join him.

A number of U.S. racetracks now use their own security personnel along with state commission investigators instead of the TRPB. Still, the security standards established by the TRPB are recognized internationally as highly effective in terms of wagering integrity and security. And believe me, through the years there has been no lack of work for the TRPB and other investigative bodies.

During my earliest years on the backstretch I witnessed all sorts of nefarious behavior, even with the high-profile presence of the TRPB. In those more carefree days, putting over a fast one was considered part of the game, even admired, or at least greeted with a wink and a nod by those in the know. Fortunately, times have changed. Today there is a high priority to detect and deal with activities that erode confidence in the sport.

For example, some jockeys did not hesitate to use a "machine" – a small, low volt electrical device – to shock an un-

Genuine Risk made a believer out of trainer LeRoy Jolley.

responsive horse into a burst of energy. Conversely, I watched jockeys of extraordinary ability discourage their mounts in an effort to set up a subsequent effort to cash a bet, compromising their talent through dishonest tactics. This told me they were more interested in stealing a dollar than earning a hundred on the square.

Such behavior often went unpunished, in part due to the precarious nature of the jockey profession and the low expectations of income from the paltry purse structure of the day. Then, as now, the top ten percent among jockeys won ninety percent of the money, with the others scrambling after the rest. This has become less of a problem in recent years as tracks have healthier purse structures and fees for unplaced mounts have been raised, thus providing enough incentive for riders always to put forth their best efforts.

Neither were trainers of bygone eras above delving into all sorts of questionable methods to manipulate the outcome of a race.

"Speedballs" were a concoction of cocaine and heroin known to motivate a horse that had slipped in performance. One speedball and nagging ailments were temporarily forgotten, allowing a horse to run pain-free – and his people to cash. Later, of course, the pain returned, sometimes worse than before.

In a particularly heinous scheme, a small round sponge could be shoved up a horse's nostril, inhibiting breathing just enough to keep a favorite off the board.

Trainers would regularly allow their private veterinarians to "tap" the joints of horses in order to remove excess fluid from inflammation. This would be done the day before a race, and after a couple of hours with their legs in a tub of ice, those horses felt no pain, at least long enough to run.

In wide use even before it became a legal medication, the diuretic Lasix enables horses to breathe more easily during a race, while reducing the chances of experiencing exercise induced pulmonary hemorrhage, aka "bleeding." Lasix also has the effect of allowing a horse who bleeds to continue racing rather than spend unproductive months at a farm. On the other hand, Lasix is considered by many to belong to the group of medications which are called "performance enhancing," as well as being able to mask illegal drugs through dilution of urine. Starting in 2020, North American tracks began to phase out legal Lasix use in younger horses, a trend that many industry leaders hoped would lead to a "drug free" era in racing.

Certain forms of anabolic steroids were legal in racehorses until their use was curtailed in the 21st century. Designer drugs, like the potent narcotic analgesic Sublimaze, were immediately illegal and used at a trainer's risk, not to mention the horse's. Throughout the 1980s and '90s, the sport was plagued by "milkshaking," a bicarbonate of soda treatment close to race time that retarded muscle fatigue. There also has been a persistent use of bronchodilators like clenbuterol and albuterol, which eventually became more strictly regulated.

In the past, authorities did what they could to discourage illegal drug use in racehorses, but the pervading sentiment was, "If they don't test for it, it's okay." For many decades, drug testing was done by saliva tests, which is why the post-race collection area is called the "spit barn." Testing of both blood and urine has evolved with the advent mass spectrometry and gas chromatography, to the point where traces of illegal or controlled substances can be measured down to the nanogram, or one-millionth of a gram. Nonetheless, these illegal substances, often referred to as "designer" drugs or "juice," have accounted for inexplicable success by previously unsuccessful trainers and are currently the bane of the sport. Even a miniscule trace can result in severe repercussions for the trainer as the ultimate insurer of the condition of the horse, not to mention forfeiture of purse money by owners.

In my naïve youth, I also came to learn that horse sales operated in a very different world from the racetrack, and that they were definitely not under the jurisdiction of the TRPB, or comparable enforcers. At sales, my eyes were opened to a fresh set of Runyonesque characters thriving in an unregulated atmosphere replete with wildcatters, treasure hunters, and sophisticated grifters.

By the time I made a foray into the auction world in the winter of 1982, at the Hialeah yearling sale in Florida, I was well aware of the mines in the minefield. The moment I stepped onto the scene, I was offered a kick-back of five percent on any horses I could encourage my boss to purchase. I should have been shocked that the offer came from one of the principals of the sales company, but I wasn't. Alas, such bald-faced thievery has never been among my many other vices, which is why I found myself passing on that offer and many more through the years. But I paid close attention, if for no other reason than in the name of self-preservation.

One of the most common ploys at a Thoroughbred auction is for an individual to approach the seller with the following proposition: "Set a price and I'll guarantee you get it. We split anything over that number fifty-fifty." Obviously, in such an arrangement some buyer is getting set up as the patsy, paying over the honest price and providing hefty profits for the scammers in charge.

The next most popular hustle requires a cooperative underbidder, or shill, in the employ of the scammer who runs up the bidding, while the scammer encourages his client to keep going as the bid rises well past what otherwise would have been an honest price for the horse in question.

Product tampering also was a common practice. I have seen anemic horse tails braided with extensions, scars painted over, joints injected, problem knees surgically stapled, and shins scraped – all in an effort to make a young horse more attractive than he should be, for at least those moments of scrutiny during a sales experience. At one yearling sale, I checked on an attractive colt I'd seen at the farm, notable for his chewed-off tail (common among playful yearlings) and was shocked to see a long, flowing tail. They had skillfully woven in an extension that you couldn't tell from the real thing. Fortunately, as the 21st century unfolded, such practices began falling out of general favor as sales companies attempted to guarantee the integrity of the process to prospective buyers.

Let's not fool ourselves, though. Where there is money to be made, some individuals will take any edge they can get, and the naïve first-timer wishing to dip a toe might as well be stepping into shark-infested waters. Even though there are rules in horse racing, the sport remained a largely unregulated business, at least on a national scale. Beyond the individual state racing commissions with their varying sets of rules, Thoroughbred racing had no central governing body and no all-powerful commissioner who could enforce universal rules and behaviors.

The problems of a lack of centralized governance have been further exacerbated by the independence of racetrack ownership conglomerates. Until the 2000s, a majority of racetracks were individually owned and operated by sole proprietorships. The DeBartolo family did own several second and third tier tracks in the 1970s and '80s, but until Frank Stronach created Magna Entertainment Corporation in 1999, track owners were completely independent from one another, with no obligation to cooperate on running dates, stakes scheduling, or marketing.

Under the MEC corporate banner, Stronach went on a track-buying binge, acquiring Gulfstream Park, Pimlico, Laurel, Golden Gate Fields, Bay Meadows, Santa Anita Park, Lone Star Park, Remington Park, Portland Meadows, and Thistledown, along with the standardbred tracks The Meadows and Flamboro Downs, as well as the Multnomah dog track. Eventually, Magna had to shed some of those properties, before finally declaring bankruptcy in 2009. A privately held company called The Stronach Group rose from the ashes to purchase the best of those tracks, and by 2020 TSG still owned properties in California, Maryland, and Florida. Headed by Frank's daughter Belinda Stronach, the company also owned the XpressBet wagering platform and track bet processor AmTote as well, rebranded later under their 1/ST banner.

Churchill Downs Inc. leveraged its premier attraction, the Kentucky Derby, into a gaming company that expanded to own racetracks in Florida, Louisiana, and Illinois, along with a number of casinos. New York's three principal racetracks – Belmont, Aqueduct, Saratoga – are run as a regional monopoly by the New York Racing Association, a quasi-governmental operation.

So there it is. The Stronach Group tracks are in business to benefit the Stronach family. The publicly-traded Churchill Downs Inc. must pledge its fealty first and foremost to its shareholders. And the NYRA answers to their masters in halls of state government in Albany.

Such divided loyalties among the most powerful racetrack ownerships have discouraged any significant degree of national unity, the kind enjoyed by other professional sports. The resulting lack of a single set of rules for medication or other infractions has plagued horse racing for years and likely will continue until something happens to force the issue of a national governing body and office of commissioner.

In 2020, the U.S. Congress passed the Horse Racing Integrity Act (HISA), designed to address the absence of unified national standards in drug testing, penalties, and enforcement, with its implementation scheduled for 2022. Time will tell how effective HISA can be.

Like many other enterprises, the Thoroughbred game is a cyclical business, subject to peaks and valleys over the long term, many of them due to circumstances outside of and unrelated to the industry.

With an estimated 7.2 million horses in the U.S. - including 3.1 million for recreation, 1.2 million for showing, 1.2 million for racing and over 500,000 working – the American Horse Council Foundation's 2017 National Economic Impact Study estimated the industry's direct contribution to the U.S. economy to exceed $50 billion. That's billion, with a capital "B." The industry's ancillary effects on other sectors of the economy resulted in a total contribution at $122 billion and a total employment impact of 1.7 million jobs.

In 1984, The Jockey Club reported that the foal crop in North America was 49,247. From that point, the production level of Thoroughbred horses began a slide to a projected 2022 foal crop of 18,700. At the same time, the average earnings of a racehorse in 1990 was $8,680, while the 2018 average earnings per horse was $24,223. These figures are most important when one considers two things: supply and demand, as well as the cost of maintenance (see Appendix 1).

The industry grew by leaps and bound through the 1960s and throughout the '70s as savvy accountants pushed their clients to take advantage of the tax provisions that allowed multiple deductions for investment in racehorses and full deductions for the expense of maintaining them. For many, the tax laws provided almost free investment when applied against ordinary earnings, basically throwing a party hosted by Uncle Sam.

In 1986, the party was over when the Tax Reform Act dealt a severe blow to horse racing, eliminating many of the advantageous methods of expensing and depreciating assets, and turning horses that were once assets into liabilities. The net result of this was to chase away many existing and potential horse buyers and drive them to real estate and more conventional investments.

The market was also severely affected when the two primary buyers of North American bloodstock, the Coolmore/Sangster consortium and Sheikh Mohammed bin Rashid al Maktoum, decided to call a truce in their high stakes competition in 1985 and instead join forces. Only once thereafter was the yearling market to see an astounding example of the auction market at work when a trio of owners represented by trainer Wayne Lukas – Robert French, Mel Hatley, and Eugene Klein – teamed up to drive the Irish to a final bid of $13.1 million for a son of Nijinsky II out of My Charmer. The half-brother to Triple Crown winner Seattle Slew never lived up to his price tag, capturing only a couple of minor stakes races in Europe before being retired to an undistinguished career at stud. He wound up in Germany, the equivalent of an NBA first round draft choice ending his playing days in Tibet.

By 2000, when the foal crop had dropped back to 36,700, the industry responded, in part, by creating a central body called the National Thoroughbred Racing Association, specifically for the purpose of marketing the sport to the public.

From that point, yearling sales averages climbed steadily and prices for breeding stock by 2018 reached all-time highs. At the Fasig-Tipton 2019 sale of two-year-olds in training at Gulfstream Park, a son of Curlin fetched a record $3.65 million. The stallion's stud fee was $100,000.

Make no mistake about it, a racehorse cannot be considered an asset until it proves otherwise. Until then it is a liability, necessitating daily upkeep, and certainly not liquid. It is certainly valid to question the logic of paying $3.65 million for an unraced Thoroughbred, even though total purses for 2018 were $1.1 billion, up roughly 80 percent from twenty years previously. Annual training costs for a racehorse at a tier one or two track are conservatively $40,000-$50,000. This means that if someone pays more than $250,000 for a potential race-horse, they are making the following statement: This animal will be a stakes horse, or at least a superior runner, capable of earning back his purchase price and the equivalent of two years' worth of expenses.

With more purse money offered and fewer horses racing for those purses, the conclusion could be drawn that things are getting easier. That might be correct – if it wasn't for the many unpredictable variables attached to the Thoroughbred game, as well as some hard numbers.

Yes, foal crops are down. But the price of horses offered at sales has increased, and not proportionately. Yes, purses have increased. But the number of races run annually has decreased and therefore so has the number of opportunities to win that purse money. The Jockey Club Fact Book, which can be found on TJC's website, is the place to find the numbers and trends behind such contradictions, as well as other statistics relative to the industry.

They will invariably lead, however, to what will be our recurrent theme in the ideal investment approach, i.e., the goal always should be to acquire quality, quality, quality.

Jess Jackson (above) and Satish Sanan, men of ideas

CHAPTER 3

PLAYING A TEAM GAME

"I was born at night, but it wasn't last night."
~ T. Boone Pickens

If you listen to no other advice, please heed the following words of the late, great Arnold Kirkpatrick, the Eclipse Award-winning writer and publisher of the *Thoroughbred Record* whose wisdom and encouragement did much to inspire the creation of this book:

"Don't check your brains at the stable gate!"

In a game at which vast fortunes have been made and lost in a short period of time, there is no substitute for two things: experience and honesty. Take my word for it, or learn the hard way.

When I first began working at the racetrack in Florida in the early 1970s, there was a trainer who led the standings and kept a high profile. He drove a flashy Cadillac and sported an expensive wardrobe. I asked him how he got started in the business, and he told an interesting tale.

He was originally a bail-bondsman, and as happens in that business, he was stiffed on a $5,000 bond when an accused client fled the jurisdiction. In lieu of the lost bond, he ended up with a Thoroughbred racehorse for the $5,000. Whether or not it was worth $5,000 remained to be seen.

He was not in the least interested in pursuing the racing game, so he lured a prospective buyer to the barn at Gulfstream Park in hopes of recouping his loss. The buyer, however, said he was not interested in a horse so cheaply valued. He asked if there was another, priced to reflect higher quality. The bondsman said, "Sure, if you insist," and told the groom to take the $5,000 horse back to its stall. After a few moments, the groom led out the same horse wearing a different halter.

"This one's ten-grand," the bondsman declared, and the buyer agreed to the price. The former bondsman had found a new calling.

In 1997, a new face appeared at the Keeneland July yearling sale. Satish Sanan was a native of India who emigrated to England when he was 16 and went on to make his fortune in computers and eventually health care as founder and CEO of IMR Global and Zavata Healthcare Services. At that point he decided to fulfill his lifelong dream of owning Thoroughbred horses. He proceeded to buy a half dozen yearlings at that first Keeneland foray, then continued to invest millions over the ensuing years.

Sanan's Padua Stable was rewarded quickly for his investments. He won the 1998 Breeders' Cup Juvenile Fillies with Cash Run, a $1.2 million yearling purchase, and took Grade I victories with Yes Its True and Exchange Rate. Not content with simple ownership, Sanan purchased the former Brookside Training Center in Ocala, Fla., formerly owned by the late aerospace magnate Allen Paulson. Sanan staffed his new acquisition with excellent horsemen and invested close to $30 million in state-of-the-art improvements, including innovations he observed at other facilities around the world. At its peak of operation, the Padua Thoroughbred operation put 50 to 60 two-year-olds in training every year.

In 2007, Sanan revised his business plan and announced that Padua was dispersing or relocating its Florida-based stallions and breeding stock. Then he purchased the former Bluegrass Heights Farm in Lexington, Ky.

At that point, Sanan had previously been sole proprietor of all Padua investments. His subsequent decision to join forces with Jess Jackson's Stonestreet Stable proved to be a turning point for Sanan in many ways, especially in the co-ownership of Curlin, a two-time Horse of the Year and highly promising stallion prospect.

Backgrounds aside, Sanan and Jackson, an international wine baron, had many things in common other than their entrepreneurial acumen. In their Thoroughbred investments, they both harbored feelings that they had been compromised along the way by unethical advisors and agents. Both men set out to rectify what they considered this Achilles heel of the business.

Sanan made his attack via an aggressive media presence, while Jackson used the civil court system. Neither one hesitated to point fingers at former associates for what they considered such practices as double-dealing and undisclosed payoffs at the sales. Sanan cited numerous instances while investing over $100 million in the sport when various schemes had siphoned away commissions without his knowledge. In response, he established the Alliance of Industry Reform, which led to changes in the auction process to protect buyers from such practices as double agency.

Sanan was elected to the Breeders' Cup board of directors, where he became the most vocal of the organization's members. Predictably, he rubbed many of his fellow directors the wrong way when he questioned their non-democratic and secretive methodology. Sanan made his points, however, before leaving the Breeders' Cup board and eventually selling his farms and his horses.

Jackson made his mark on the beverage industry in the 1980s when he first marketed an affordable white wine to bridge the gap between the ultra-premium and cheaper products with his Kendall-Jackson Chardonnay. So popular was his wine that by the time of his death in 2011 his winery was ranked the ninth largest in the U.S., producing five million cases of wine annually, and Jackson was ranked by Forbes as the 536th richest person in the world.

Under his Stonestreet Stable banner, Jackson made nearly as impressive a mark in Thoroughbred racing as not only the principal owner of Curlin, but also Rachel Alexandra, the filly who reigned as Horse of the Year in 2009.

Jackson also raised industry havoc when he decided some of the advisors involved in his Thoroughbred holdings were taking advantage of him. In 2005, he filed suit in California Superior Court in San Diego against three former advisors, alleging fraudulent misrepresentation, breach of fiduciary duty, and unjust enrichment in his purchase of horses, both privately and at public sales. Naming bloodstock agent Emmanuel de Seroux, de Seroux's Narvick International and Continental Bloodstock companies, trainer Bruce Headley, and racing manager Brad Martin, Jackson claimed they steered him to horses on which they had negotiated secret deals to inflate prices, while taking secret commissions and profits of over $3.2 million.

The fact that such alleged practices had been either ignored or quietly excused through the years made Jackson even more determined to expose those who profited, and his litigation made an impact. The suit was settled two years later, one week before the trial was to begin, when de Seroux agreed to pay Jackson $3.5 million, and Headley and Martin settled for $900,000 and $250,000, respectively, to end the dispute. The settlement was in effect a negotiated peace, which found no admission of any fault or wrongdoing by either party, according to Jackson's attorney.

Even though Jackson and Sanan played at the highest levels of the sport, and their platforms were powerful, the message they delivered for all Thoroughbred investors is clear: Always seek good, honest advice from professional, reputable horsemen who will communicate with you, be it your advisor, bloodstock agent, or pedigree expert. There is a long list of hugely successful business and professional people who have come and gone from the Thoroughbred ranks because they were either too careless in choosing their advisors or decided they were astute enough to go it on their own. Although they hired the top minds in their chosen professions, when it came to racing they might trust in someone lacking the talent and scruples to be entrusted with millions of dollars for selecting and/or training their racing stock.

Despite its casual appearance, the abundance of pastoral settings and home-spun adages, the Thoroughbred business can be as complex as any you may experience. Please understand that you cannot acquire the degree of knowledge you will need to succeed in a short period of time without making it a full-time occupation. As a novice horse owner remarked to me upon having been duped once or twice, "Damn, these lessons are expensive."

In order to increase the chance you will choose the right advisor for your racing enterprise, and thus make those lessons not quite so expensive, consider the following:

Rule No. 1: Anyone you consider retaining as an advisor should be willing to provide references. You should take the time to check those references thoroughly.

Rule No. 2: Depending on the level of participation, make sure your budget allows for consulting fees for the necessary advisors and related services (pedigree analysis, heart scans, gait analysis, etc.). Keep in mind that racing is a tremendously complex endeavor with a constant flow of information and data that your advisor should be able to assimilate and interpret it accurately for your benefit. They should be able to identify trends and anticipate the market. A talented, experienced professional will see the handwriting on the wall before you will.

Rule No. 3: Don't let appearances deceive you. It is fine for a potential advisor to have an extensive library of industry related tomes and be well-versed in the history of the game, but you should take the person with boots-on-the-ground experience every time.

Keep in mind that in the early days of your venture you will need to devote a considerable amount of time to learn the basics, even though you might think you already know most of them. Pick an advisor with whom you would like to spend time even if you weren't delving into the horse game. Compatibility counts, especially when you're paying for dinner most of the time.

Romantic notions to the contrary, most of the men and women involved at the highest levels of racing can be seriously focused individuals, some to the point of obsession. That is why, when it comes to advisors and trainers, the investor should expect a high degree of communication. Trainers who fail at this basic practice have paid the price, like the fellow at Monmouth who forgot to tell his owner his horse was entered in a particular race. When the horse galloped home first, the trainer received a call the next day, informing him who the new trainer was and where to deliver the rest of his horses – a vivid reality check as to who the horse belongs to and who pays the bills.

Rule No. 4: Always ask questions. And there are no stupid questions, especially at the outset of a new enterprise. The horse racing game uses its own vernacular, and many terms are indecipherable without help (see the Glossary provided later in this book). Be prepared to feel like an outsider in most conversations until you pick up the lingo, and the sooner the better. And beware – anyone who attempts to make you feel inadequate because you don't yet speak the language is not looking out for your interests.

Once you know the qualities to look for in an advisor, it is time to be more specific, based on your own personal experience, the amount of your investment, and the amount of personal involvement you anticipate. You will need to decide if you want a general advisor, or a bloodstock agent, or both, or an even more extensive team that includes a pedigree expert and a veterinarian. You should also factor in whether you wish to race or breed – or both – which leads to further decisions on choosing a trainer and boarding farm. Then there is the necessity of involving an accountant with knowledge of the Thoroughbred industry, rather than relying on your current accountant or lawyer to educate themselves in the intricacies of the horse business.

Bloodstock agents make their living as middlemen, taking a commission when buying and selling horses. Their function can be as simple as that, with the agent taking the industry standard five percent from the principal (you) for advising on the selection of a horse and either negotiating the private purchase or bidding at auction on your behalf. Many bloodstock agents are also a good source of advice regarding matings, trainers, farms, and stallion shares, but a cautionary note is appropriate at this stage – since the bloodstock agent makes his living buying and selling, there can be a "churn" problem when they are more interested in short-term turnover rather than meeting your long-term goals.

A general advisor can also be your bloodstock agent, working exclusively for you. They will assist in setting up your business plan, closely monitor your progress, and keep your program on course. Usually this requires an agreement which includes a retainer and may or may not include incentives such as a percentage of any profits or, in the case of stallions, a breeding right.

Serving as the focal point for your team, the advisor can scrutinize individual bills and see that you and your accountant deal with only one total billing per month rather than a raft of individual invoices. Also, your general advisor

Bloodstock agents inspect yearlings at Keeneland.

should be able to arrange for your visits to the track and the sales, as well as manage any stable business not assumed by your trainer.

The idea of partnership with your advisor appeals to investors who like their team members to have "skin in the game." But it can be a slippery slope, depending on who has control of the decision making. I have seen such partnerships go wrong more often than marriages, and some breakups can turn extremely acrimonious. When you are used to making unilateral decisions, any pushback from an advisor/partner may turn into finger-pointing and blaming.

The key to success and tranquility lies in the amount of trust and friendship established between the partners, although one piece of advice is universal: Always put it in writing! (More on this in Chapter 8.)

The newcomer to horse ownership also must be prepared for a great deal of tedious paperwork. You will need someone you can rely on to handle licensing, subscriptions, and information requests from both individual racing organizations and government bodies. Each state has its own requirements for owner and stable licensing, even requiring fingerprints with each state application and renewal. As if your fingerprints would change!

Fortunately, there is an organization called the National Racing Compact, which may have been the best kept secret in racing for the past 30 years. The creators of the Compact identified roadblocks to a universal license as the different criminal history criteria used by each state in determining eligibility requirements for obtaining each state's license, and the fact that sharing of criminal history information between racing jurisdictions generally is not permitted. In its effort to streamline the licensing system, the literature of the National Racing Compact states:

"The vast majority of license applicants have no criminal history. For those participants, a plan was needed to simplify the licensing process, which often is time consuming, expensive, complicated and duplicative, thereby reducing the regulatory burden on a majority of the participants who race in multiple states.

"The National Racing Compact was created as an independent, interstate governmental entity, composed of pari-mutuel racing regulators from participating states, which has been authorized by the states and approved by the Federal Bureau of Investigation to receive criminal history information from the FBI.

"The Compact is empowered to set standards for individual licenses, accept applications and fingerprints, analyze criminal history information and issue a national license which will be recognized by all member states and other states that may elect to recognize the license. Participants need only to complete one license application and provide one set of fingerprints instead of duplicating the license process in each state. Once approved for the national license, a participant then pays only a participation fee in each state in which the national licensee wishes to race."

Makes sense to me.

(See Appendix 3 for the list of participating jurisdictions. Details of the various licensing processes can be found at the NRC website, in Appendix 7.)

The legendary trainer Charlie Whittingham enjoyed teasing listeners with a well-worn quip about horse owners that went something like this:

"Treat them like mushrooms. Keep 'em in the dark and covered with plenty of shit."

For this, Charlie would get a good laugh, even from some of his high-profile owners like oilmen Nelson Bunker Hunt and Howard B. Keck, show business celebrities Greer Garson and Burt Bacharach, and racetrack mogul Marje Everett. They were hardly naïve, and yet Whittingham won so many important races for them that his folksy, politically incorrect aphorisms mattered not one bit. With their independent wealth and tax breaks, they were content with the trophies and the glory of winning those races.

Well into the 21st century, however, the Thoroughbred business is just that, a business, and subject to the same tests of honesty and fiduciary discipline as any other. If you decide to use any of the information in this book, the decision to find competent, honest, and serious advisors will be the best thing you can do. There is no longer any room for "mushroom" ownership.

Although there are no exams to qualify bloodstock agents in their chosen profession, don't assume that all agents are equal. Working as an assistant to an agent of legendary renown can be an excellent indicator of a quality "education." Because it is in their best interest to have well-advised investors, the principals at the major auction sales houses are always willing to identify such agent prospects. It is a profession that requires more than a sales catalog and a cell phone, and although a charming foreign accent may be intriguing, it doesn't make anyone anymore skilled than anyone else.

Peter Bradley III started his bloodstock enterprise in 1995 after doing his groundwork as a hotwalker, groom, foreman, and assistant trainer on the Southern California circuit. His passion for the game led him to Kentucky, where he gained further experience as a farm manager and bloodstock agent. Bradley Thoroughbreds, LLC, has gained industry respect, trading in racehorses, broodmares, stallion shares, and stallion prospects, while sharing knowledge with clients in a broad range of industry related activities like matings, insurance, and pinhooking.

According to Bradley, his primary discussion with any prospective client concerns their personal purposes for the endeavor.

"I point out that it is a sport, and the enjoyment factor is primary," Bradley said. "Thoroughbreds are difficult to play strictly as an investment. Occasionally you hit a winning lottery ticket, but you need to be in it for the sheer joy it can provide. Paramount to any investment program is planning a strategy, both for entering and exiting. We look for Saturday horses that can compete at the top level – Belmont, Saratoga, Del Mar – and always spread the risk."

Alex Solis III was raised in a racing family with as strong a pedigree as one could wish for. His grandfather, Bert Sonnier, trained thirty-eight stakes winners, including champion Nodouble (aka The Arkansas Traveller), Funistrada, Meadow-lake, and Stage Door Betty. Alex's father, Alex Solis, Jr., is a Hall of Fame jockey and the winner of 5,035 races.

Alex III spent time working for trainers Mel Stute, Bruce Headley, and Richard Mandella before deciding on a career in bloodstock. He is a member of the Breeders' Cup Board of Directors and lives in Kentucky, where he is Director of Blood-stock and Racing for Gainesway Farm.

Jason Litt's equine education comes from work experience at Taylor Made Farm and the veterinary practice of Cheny, Northrup & Landry as well as a seven-year stint in bloodstock work at Three Chimneys Farm. He also is based in Kentucky.

Solis and Litt teamed in 2009. Their services include purchase and management of horses acquired at auction and through private negotiations, formation of racing partnerships, and breeding consultations. Their success at the highest levels came quickly with champions Shared Belief and Covfefe, two-time Breeders' Cup winner Mizdirection, and Kentucky Derby winner Country House, along with dozens of other stakes winners.

Brad Weisbord grew up in the shadow of his father Barry, founder of the *Thoroughbred Daily News* and one of the sport's most prolific innovators. In 2004, the younger Weisbord attended to the University of Wisconsin, Madison, preparing for a career in investment banking and real estate development, but when he graduated in 2008, he found his timing was terrible, landing him in the middle of the Great Recession. Not only was there a hiring freeze in the industry, but it also turned out that most real estate-based companies were laying off their best talent, so Weisbord looked to racing for an alternative career.

"Even though I grew up with a father in the business, I had never considered it the place I could make a living, but given the circumstances, I thought I should give it a look," Weisbord said.

He walked hots for trainer Alan Goldberg and worked at the *Thoroughbred Daily News* for a year. Then in 2009 he reached out to Ahmed Zayat, whose racing stable was included in his bankruptcy reorganization. Zayat hired him as his "finance and stallion manager" and soon named him racing manager, a position he held for two years until becoming COO of Barry Irwin's Team Valor International, managing a 165-horse stable with over 300 investors.

Striking out on his own in 2014, Weisbord founded BSW Bloodstock which has managed the winners of over 75 Grade I stakes, including two Triple Crown events for Sol Kumin, as well as Grade I races for Gary Barber and Michael Dubb.

It's probably safe to say Brad made the right career choice.

In 2017 Weisbord teamed up with Liz Crow to found ELITE Sales, focusing on the marketing of top-level racing and breeding stock. They sold champion mare Tepin for $8 million, putting them on the map with total sales exceeding $50 million as the 2020s dawned.

Weisbord likes to think of his approach to owners as "brutally honest," telling prospective players to consider Thoroughbreds a "sport, not a business" and they should be in it for the right reasons or don't do it at all, citing a passion for the sport as the benchmark for new investors. His philosophy, he says, is simple: "The owner gets all the credit."

Some other agents I have known over the years and deserve a nod include Donato Lanni, John Moynahan, Antony Stroud, Hugo Merry, Luke Lillingston, Will DeBurgh, Hubert

Guy, Alan Quartucci, Barry Berkelhammer, Michel Zerolo, and the Bell brothers – Reynolds and Headley – as well as David Ingordo, Kip Elser, Mike Ryan, Nick Sallusto, Patrick Lawley-Wakelin and the Young brothers, Steve and Gary. Their contacts may be found, with others, at the Keeneland website, listed in Appendix 7.

Among other active U.S. bloodstock agencies in that top tier would be the Hill 'n' Dale Sales Agency, Taylor Made Sales Agency, and the Sallusto & Albina Premier Bloodstock Agency, Denali Stud, Eaton Sales and Bluewater Sales. Dozens more can be found in *The Source* as well as the plethora of individual bloodstock agents, which are also listed on The Jockey Club's Ownerview website, and you are encouraged to sort through them until you find the one that best suits your situation.

Although a big part of the game requires a good eye for the animal, don't underestimate the importance of your horse's family. When it comes to sorting through the complex world of Thoroughbred pedigrees, do not be alarmed. There are plenty of experienced guides to help cut through the clutter. They include Ed Rosen, Sid Fernando, Bill Oppenheim, John Sparkman, and Alan Porter, among others.

Rosen first made a name for himself when he put Tale of the Cat on a short list of stallion candidates for a syndicate formed by trainer John Forbes in 1995. The son of Storm Cat went on to win $360,900, including the Grade 1 King's Bishop Stakes at Saratoga, before he was sold to the Coolmore to stand at Ashford Stud in Versailles, Ky. Tale of the Cat went on to a skyrocket career as a stallion with a highly successful international impact in both the Northern and Southern Hemispheres.

Rosen really hit the mark for client James Scatuorchio with a series of yearling purchases commencing in 1997 with More Than Ready, who became a major stakes winner and successful sire. Champion English Channel followed in 2002, and then in 2004 the yearling later known as Scat Daddy – named for his owner – capped Rosen's run with a solid racing career followed by spectacular success at stud that included his son, Triple Crown winner Justify.

When Vitamin Water founder Mike Repole decided to take on the Thoroughbred game, his first move was to assemble a top-notch team of advisors. Besides Rosen, the Repole team included veterinarian Scott Hay and trainer Todd Pletcher. Their success speaks for itself, with champion Uncle Mo, Travers Stakes winner Stay Thirsty, and Breeders' Cup Classic winner Vino Rosso among the winners they've unearthed for the Repole stable. Like many top-tier stables, they have begun to team up with their competitors when buying high-priced stallion prospects, sharing the risk while willing to share the glory of the winner's circle.

The basic methodology of the Repole team is similar to that of most of the top stables in the U.S., beginning with a business plan and budget for the year. There follows an in-depth screening of the pedigrees in the appropriate books (such as Keeneland's yearling sales catalogs arranged by quality), group inspection of the yearlings on the broad list, and a veterinary opinion on those who pass scrutiny as the team decides on the short list.

From that point, they assign a range of relative values to the remaining yearlings (or two-year-olds at certain sales) and decide how high to bid on each individual. Should they become interested in a potentially multi-million-dollar horse, another decision is made as to whether they should battle alone or partner up with a potential rival.

While there are a lot of very good bloodstock agents, the horse business has long been the playing field for many charlatans, principally because so few people know a lot about the business, and because there is a huge luck factor involved. The charm and mystery of the game also provides a fertile ground for hustlers and grifters to seduce new participants bringing fresh money. The lack of a centralized governing body with jurisdiction over sales company policy, along with the lack of peer oversight groups, contributes to possible malfeasance. So, remember the lesson of Rule No. 1: Do not assume that anyone's credentials are sterling unless you see proof in writing and receive verification of their integrity from multiple sources.

I repeat myself, but for good reason. Honesty in the game is the paramount commodity. Your advisor should be willing and available to answer your questions openly and candidly. As Rule No. 4 explains, successful people in other businesses are reluctant to appear stupid by asking a lot of questions about the horse business. Ask first, verify second, trust later.

The price of good advice? I'd like to say "priceless," and in the long run that might be true. In raw terms, figure on a five percent commission for horses selected on your behalf, and the same five percent for horses sold on your behalf. Question anyone that proposes a higher fee, since this is the industry standard and has been for a long time. Most agents will agree to a sliding scale that further reduces this percentage when prices get to seven figures. In lieu of commissions, you can retain a good advisor for a monthly or annual flat fee, with kickers as incentives.

Also customary in the business is the granting of a breeding right when a good colt turns out to make the grade as a stallion. The deserving individuals could include the trainer, bloodstock agent, and farm manager, depending on the involvement they had in the horse's development and success. A breeding right is the entitlement to bring one mare each season to be covered by the stallion, at no cost to the right holder, but does not include any actual ownership in the stallion. This breeding right is not the same as a stallion share, which is actual ownership equity in the stallion via a syndicate.

A share entitles the shareholder to breed at least one mare per season and derive a portion of any other income from the horse. Whereas the shareholder contributes to the maintenance of the horse and may sell that share (while giving right of first refusal to the other syndicate members) and insures the share based on the entire value of the animal, the right holder has no responsibility for the horse's general costs but also does not participate in any dividends such as a portion of receipts from the sale of extra breedings over the normal book of mares. A breeding right might sometimes be saleable as well, depending on the syndicate agreement, and usually will bring 40-50 percent of a share price.

Keep in mind when budgeting for auctions that the sales company also will charge sellers five percent. It does not matter if their horses are sold or fail to make their reserve price and are returned to the seller. The seller is allowed to commit to an amount at which they will take their horse home, a situation identified in the published sales results as RNA or "Reserve Not Attained." But many times, horses do not sell because the seller has unrealistic expectations of the market and sets their reserve too high. Immediately after the horse leaves the auction ring, reality sets in and they are faced with taking their asset home, thereby achieving zero cash flow, not the best situation for those in the commercial market.

Most sales companies now provide a window for potential purchasers to bid on published RNAs, either in person or online, while the seller retains the option of refusing any such offers. Over the past few years, online bids for RNAs have become a popular method for these post-sale transactions. The result page on the sales company website will have "make bid" in the price column, and buyers can submit their offer which will be passed on to the seller for consideration.

Usually, a post-auction bid of 80-85 percent of the stated reserve will make a deal float. Sometimes even a lower stab will work, especially if the horse has a minor flaw or a veterinary issue. Factor in the reality that many horses will develop problems in training, and you may wish to use this method of bargaining to mitigate possible losses. Your veterinarian will be able to help you in this process, keeping in mind that the issue that might keep a horse from bring top dollar at auction may well eventually be inconsequential in respect to that horse's racing career. The history of the game is littered with examples of horses that had fractures, ailments, or questionable airways and "failed the vet," yet went on to achieve stellar records on the track. I once questioned a vet about a horse we passed on at the sales for a sketchy throat. His response?

"They change."

Yearling auctions represent the ultimate in horse shopping.

CHAPTER 4

THE BUYING GAME

"If you want to be in the movies, you'll have to go to Hollywood. If you want to be in the horse business, you'll have to go to Kentucky."
                                          ~ Anonymous racetracker

For some reason, Americans are fascinated by auctions. They bid against each other for dinner dates, for antiques displayed on Fifth Avenue or found in the hayloft of a barn. They raise their hands for real estate someone else can't afford, for cars they lusted after in their youth, and for Andy Warhol's painting of soup cans, paying millions upon millions of dollars.

Perhaps this is true because it seems like it's the American way that everything is always for sale. As a certain President proclaimed, a hundred years ago, "The business of America is business."

This chapter will help the investor satisfy that desire to own a racehorse, a luxury item if there ever was one. There will be information on the methods of acquisition, whether through private purchase, claiming, or buying at public auction. There are a number of rules worth following, including a few that have never changed since the dawn of horse trading.

The first and foremost rule will always be: Buy quality horses, quality pedigrees, and sound individuals.

In terms of what you will pay for quality, there are unpredictable factors that influence price. These can include prevailing economic conditions, the stock market, unstable world events, or fluctuations in the value of the dollar. Commercial Thoroughbred value is driven by supply and demand for those horses with recognizable quality either in their pedigree, their physical conformation, or their proven racing ability.

To facilitate the passion to purchase at public auctions, there is Park Bernet and Sotheby's for art, antiques, and real estate. For high-end automobiles, there is Mecum, Barrett Jackson, and Hemmings. And for racehorses, that ultimate item of luxury, there are the major Northern Hemisphere sales companies of Keeneland, Fasig-Tipton, and Ocala Breeders Sales in the U.S., Goffs and Tattersalls in Ireland and the United Kingdom, and Arqana in France.

If you are going to be a serious student of the game and plan to invest a substantial sum of money, you should also be willing to invest some time as well, just as you would for any other business venture. Various parts of the Thoroughbred business may not seem to be related, but if you keep at it long enough, you'll find an underlying principle exists.

Of great value would be participating in one of the new owner seminars conducted by The Jockey Club, the National Thoroughbred Racing Association, and the Thoroughbred Owners and Breeders Association, the major advocacy groups that offer valuable resources to the prospective racehorse investor. New owner seminars held at various locations around the country, usually in conjunction with big events such as Breeders' Cup or the Triple Crown races. There are many advantages to attending, primarily because you will be among a group of people with the same interests and a similar knowledge base, asking the questions pertinent to this new endeavor. You will encounter instructors otherwise inaccessible to the common racing fan, as well as individuals who will be seeking to make themselves available to prospective clients in the audience.

Exposure to one of the auctions held at various locations around the world is an absolute must for the new investor. Sales of Thoroughbreds take place throughout the calendar in Florida, Kentucky, Maryland, New York, Louisiana, Texas, Washington, and California, as well as Ontario, Canada, where vendors offer specific types of horse depending on the time of year. Yearlings sell primarily in the summer and fall, broodmares and weanlings in the fall and winter, two-year-olds in training in the spring and summer. You will learn a lot by simply watching and listening to what goes on at the sales, but do not assume they are all alike. Breeding stock, yearling sales, and two-year-olds in training sales all have their own peculiarities and different casts of characters.

The Keeneland Association sales operation is head-quartered at Keeneland Race Course in Lexington, Ky. The Fasig-Tipton Company also has its headquarters in Lexington, as well as satellite locations in Saratoga Springs, N.Y., during the summer Saratoga meet, in the Baltimore area during the Preakness meet, and in Hallandale, Fla., during the Gulfstream winter meet. Fasig-Tipton also conducts sales in California and other limited venues in Louisiana, Arkansas, and Texas.

The Ocala Breeders Sales Company is the major sales venue for horses bred in Florida, conducting their sales on a schedule which mirrors but does not conflict with Keeneland and Fasig-Tipton. These sales present the top grade of yearlings, mares and foals, and two-year-olds in training, attracting serious buyers from all over the world. Minor sales companies sell locally-bred and "non-select" horses in British Columbia, Iowa, Minnesota, and Colorado. All the sales companies will send along their catalogs upon request and at no cost, although they are also available online through the useful Equineline.com Catalog iPad App now popular with many sales goers.

Yearling sales held from July through September are the source for a large percentage of North American and European racehorses, these auctions comprise the bulk of Thoroughbreds sold annually and are categorized in three grades: Preferred or Select, Open, and Restricted.

The Preferred or Select yearling sales are comprised of horses that have been inspected by a team of experts working for their respective sales companies. The yearlings are rated from A+ down to C. Yearlings rated A or B will comprise most of the Keeneland and Fasig-Tipton catalogs. Of course, they will not all be perfect individuals. Some may have minor conformational defects, but they will possess solid, commercial pedigrees. As in any similar situation, beauty is in the eye of the beholder. As a result, the price becomes whichever the braver of two final bidders is willing to pay.

Open sales will have several B-rated individuals but will be filled primarily with those rated C and those with lesser regarded pedigrees. Restricted sales are generally for state-bred yearlings and attract local buyers for racing at smaller tracks.

A warning: Never believe anyone who tells you they can predict the price of a certain horse at an individual sale, unless, of course, they have inside information as to the reserve bid on record with the sales company. And that number is usually as well-guarded as the nuclear codes.

Also, keep in mind that the horse you purchase at the yearling sales is still unbroken, untrained and has a long way to go. You will go through six to nine months of exercising patience and paying training bills before you can expect to see your horse in the walking ring with a jockey astride wearing your silks.

Two-year-olds in training sales are held from February through June and are an excellent source of runners closer to the races. The Fasig-Tipton sale held at Gulfstream Park is the premier venue of this type.

Since these horses are theoretically only 60-90 days from the races and have been scrutinized by the best horsemen in the game, the price levels are correspondingly higher than those paid for younger stock. The advantage is that you can see how horses breeze or gallop, rather than simply watch them walk at the yearling sales. Many two-year-olds are "pinhooks" that were purchased as yearlings specifically for resale as ready runners the following year. The savviest pinhookers have rolled the dice and hit home runs with selling prices many times the cost of their original investment.

There are those who distain the auctions of two-year-olds in training, feeling that horses which have yet to reach their actual second birthday are not sufficiently mature to withstand the rigors of the heavy training required to produce the fast breezing workouts that sellers hope will bring the big money. My personal preference is for two-year-old sale horses to be trained up to a good gallop, nothing more, and then leave the serious training to my trainer once I have secured the horse.

Mixed or broodmare and foal sales are sometimes combined with horses of racing age sales which are held from October through March, mainly to accommodate the breeding season which begins in early February. These sales are a source of breeding stock for those wanting to produce Thoroughbreds for future racing or sale. Pinhookers seek weanlings or horses that have just turned yearlings (referred to as "short" yearlings) to resell at the yearling sales later the same year, or they will be looking for yearlings to resell at the two-year old auctions.

Breeders with new stallions also purchase mares at the mixed sales in order to supplement their bookings in case the public demand is tepid. The standard for a syndicated stallion's book of mares calls for one or two mares for each of the shareholders, two to four mares for the standing farm, perhaps a mare or two for the trainer, and even one for a jockey considered important in the stallion's racing career.

For instance, Northern Dancer, a foal of 1961, was owned by a 34-member syndicate and produced just over 32 foals per

The influence of Northern Dancer is everlasting.

year, on average. This exclusivity contributed to the price of his offspring and the ascent of his stud fee, which at one point in the 1980s reached $1 million with no guarantee of pregnancy to the owner of the mare.

I happened to be the successful bidder for that season, on behalf of Due Process Stable in my role as general manager. The resultant foal, born on July 4, was a filly named Air Dancer, and she became a stakes winner in one of the first Maryland Million Day events. Though never worth the purchase price of her sire's stud fee, she earned $123,000 at the races and brought $750,000 when sold later as a broodmare.

Today's advanced technology enables breeding farms to judge the precise time of the mare's ovulation and thereby increase fertility rates. In stallion management, the key factor is not the number of mares a stud can breed, but the amount of covers it takes for him to impregnate each mare. If a stallion's fertility rate is 70 percent and that technology enables him to breed 100 mares and improve to 90 percent in foal, the return on investment per share price is significantly higher.

As the 21st century progressed, the books of many popular stallions soared to more than 200. However, in the spring of 2020 The Jockey Club adopted a rule that would limit a stallion to 140 mares, beginning with future stallions foaled that year. Clearly, it would take some time to gauge the impact of such a restriction. Still, 140 is a long way from Northern Dancer's 32.

Attending the sales, it will be necessary to know how to read the catalog, since the pedigree found on the page is the most relevant factor to the value of a horse. Armed with facts, the buyer can be defended against the myriad of unsubstantiated "through the grapevine" rumors and worthless scuttlebutt that serves as background noise at any auction. Be prepared to enlist a veterinarian on your behalf, since horses at most sales are sold "As Is." Relevant information – have they undergone invasive joint surgery, surgery of the upper respiratory tract or abdomen, been found to be a cribber (windsucker), or a wobbler (a neurological condition), stall-walker or have any eye issues, or are a twin – must be revealed. Otherwise, if subsequently discovered the buyer has grounds to return the horse and cancel the purchase within the time noted in the conditions of sale. Most of these issues are either announced from the auctioneer's podium or noted via the repository, where prospective buyers are able to have X-rays and airway reports examined by their veterinarian. Buyers then have the opportunity to accept the horse if they consider the issues worth whatever degree of risk they represent.

The potential buyer must be familiar with the conditions of sale, prominently included in the front of every catalog. Even if you are not inclined to read small print, this is one time you need to make an exception. Obviously, the conditions are written by the sales company attorneys and contain some technical language, but if you are not at least familiar with the terms, you may be leaving yourself open to aggravation and financial jeopardy.

Sales catalogs are a source of other valuable information, such as advertisements for agents, transport and equine insurance, farm contacts, and future sales dates, as well as hotels and restaurants close to sales venues. Most catalogs also include maps of the immediate area, along with a schematic of the sales grounds, handy for your first venture.

As noted previously, The Jockey Club's Equineline.com Catalog for iPad is a useful tool, and many buyers have taken to carrying an electronic notepad rather than, or in addition to, the traditional catalog. The online catalog has features like fingertip note-making, highlighting, and automatic updates along with results. On days when sales overlap and you find yourself inspecting horses from two catalogs, the convenience of a single iPad can be a genuine asset.

Another tool which could prove invaluable is the website of the Consignors and Commercial Breeders Association (CBA). This is a trade organization involving nearly 300 members and the only one, at least in the U.S., requiring a code of conduct. CBA's website (see Appendix 7) includes extensive information for both novices and experienced participants in racing and breeding. Their downloadable booklets, intended to dispel common misconceptions and encourage success at the sales, were produced by CBA co-founder Rob Whiteley, former director of Carl Ichan's Foxfield and breeder of 20 Grade I winners. The booklets provide insight which may save you from gaining knowledge the more expensive way, also known as experience.

Since the sales company, in return for their commission, acts as the intermediary for buyers and sellers, they are responsible for evaluating the prospective purchaser's credit. You should expect to fill out a credit application form as well as a buyer's registration, providing your billing address, banking particulars and a contact at your bank. This activity should all take place well before the auction begins, so you don't arrive at the sale ready to bid but then must wait. Although most sales companies will accept credit cards, company or cashier's checks, or wire transfers, they will allow a 15-day grace period on settling accounts.

If you have prepared your business plan correctly, you will have decided on the type of horses you will buy and the total amount you have budgeted for those purchases. Approximately one-third of an entire yearling crop will sell at auction, so there are many price levels from which to choose. The specific day of the sale you attend also will be dictated by your budget, since there is usually a pecking order to the perceived quality of the horses offered. Unless your pockets are deep, for example, you will not waste your time perusing Day 1 yearlings at the Select Keeneland Sale (average 2021 price, nearly $400,000), unless you just want to appreciate the view.

Perfectly good potential racehorses are sold throughout a given sale, and the price will decline as the auction marathon goes on. Patience is rewarded many times over if you can make your short list on the two or three days that the offerings will fall into your price range.

Competition for yearlings with the pedigree for a potential stallion has always been stiff, which is why the lots on those short lists bring multi-million-dollar bids. The record for a yearling purchase was set during the heyday of gaudy prices in 1985, when Sheikh Mohammed bin Rashid al Maktoum of Dubai paid $13.1 million for a son of Nijinsky II, winner of the English Triple Crown and a son of Northern Dancer. In 2019, Mandy Pope of Whisper Hill Farm (as well as co-owner of the Variety Wholesalers conglomerate) outbid both Sheikh Mohammed and Coolmore to set the North American high mark for a yearling filly when she paid $8.2 million for a daughter of American Pharoah. The pedigree page told everyone the filly was not only sired by a Triple Crown winner, she also was a half-sister to three-time champion Beholder and major stakes winners Into Mischief and Mendelssohn.

Such is the game at the top, and congratulations to those who can play in that giddy atmosphere. Later in a sale, as horses with less than perfect conformation and pedigree enter the sales ring, opportunity knocks. Whereas once Sheikh Mohammed's private 747 was parked at Bluegrass Airport, across the street from Keeneland, the sales pavilion parking lot becomes filled with dual-wheeled pickups and gooseneck trailers owned by Stetson-wearing cowboys. Same game, different players for different levels. The prices might be lower, but the competition for the nicest horses is just as intense.

Again, this is yet another reminder to keep your *Thoroughbred Investor's Bible* handy and stick to the rules. Here are a few more regarding sales that you should put in your notes and never forget:

-- **Insist on proper, written documentation.** If you buy a horse, require copies of foal certificates, or, in the case of European stock, passports with your ownership interest memorialized. If you do your own bidding, the sales company will send an invoice to your address, otherwise they'll send it to your agent, and they will forward to you. Sales companies require that you register and clear your credit before the sale begins. They will invoice for payment in full for purchases within 15 days and pay out proceeds within 30 days.

-- **Horse sales are exciting.** There's an electric buzz that comes from the constant movement of horses in the walking ring, scrutinized by agents and principals, the hypnotic drone of the auctioneer's chant, and the competitive back-and-forth of the bidding. There are endless theories on how best to bid at auction, and I've watched many buyers try to outmaneuver their opponents. In my experience, the optimum tactic seems to be to wait until the bidding has settled and make one bid after the two previous bidders have exhausted themselves, leaving you to step in to scoop the prize. Bid-spotters trained to recognize a wink or a nod will call out raises to the auctioneer and will help you along.

   -- *Every horse has a price, whether you are a buyer or a seller.* There is little reward in being a high bidder for the sales topper if it is not worth the price you pay. Get several opinions from your advisors and make sure you stay within your budget. It's easy to get caught up in the excitement and win a bidding battle, but no fun when you lose the war.

   Roger King was a media giant in the entertainment business and prominent Thoroughbred buyer in the 1990s, spending some of the King World money he made from launching Oprah Winfrey's career and syndicating Merv Griffin's *Wheel of Fortune* and *Jeopardy*, as well as *CSI, Survivor* and other successful television shows. King was a gregarious individual and loved the limelight, so when he attended a horse sale, he would take a seat in the first row, announce his intentions to all within earshot, and proceed to bid with a flourish, preferring to buy one for a million rather than a mere $900,000, just for the story value when he was recounting the experience later at dinner. Obviously, horse sellers loved him because he was easy to run up in price well past their expectations. However, for those who do not have "King-sized" disposable income, it's best to bid discreetly and not reveal your intentions.

   Horse auctions use a "reserve" system, whereby the seller may place a minimum price they will accept for the horse offered. If the reserve is $100,000 and the bidding stops at $95,000 the horse is listed as an RNA, for Reserve Not Attained. During the 1980s, the Due Process operation I directed was producing up to 100 foals a year. It was necessary to sell a portion of the crop for diverse reasons. Some were sold because they didn't fit the profile for tier one competition (poor conformation, weak pedigree, or unsuitable demeanor), while others went to market in order to take a profit for tax purposes or to promote our stallion interests. For most of those offered, I set the reserve at 60 percent of what I considered to be the horse's value. In that way I could either let the horse go at that price if the bidding was slow or continue bidding myself until full value was reached. Setting the price at an exact number is like deciding you know the exact hand a poker player holds. Better to set a range you can expect to land within.

--The operative word in horse sale is "sale." If you are a seller, you do not want to take horses to auction and buy them back. You will have to pay the sales company and the consignor their commissions, and still you must keep feeding that horse you wanted to sell. Sellers who stick themselves with an RNA often joke that they're now starting a racing stable, but believe me, that's the last thing they want. The farmer forced to take home his produce before it goes bad soon grows tired of eating tomatoes.

There are plenty of stories about horses that failed to make their reserve going on to successful careers. As owners are not prohibited from bidding on their own horses, many either utilize a set reserve with the sales company or participate by raising their own hand. The most notable example is the 12th Triple Crown winner, American Pharoah, who was, in effect, bought back for his breeder, Ahmed Zayat, by a bloodstock agent for $300,000. In reality, there are plenty more at every sale that sellers get stuck with when they entertain unrealistic expectations.

-- Bidding is what horse sales are all about. To have a successful sale you need both a bidder and an under-bidder, even if the latter is yourself or your reserve. I once took a son of

Horse of the Year Spectacular Bid from his first crop to Keeneland at a time when Japanese breeders were stocking up on American pedigrees. The colt had been weak and sickly, and undergone colic surgery, with scars quite visible. We considered him a poor candidate for our racing stable, although he did appear to turn the corner and looked good as a candidate for the sale. I set the reserve at $40,000, hoping to get $60,000 but willing to take the lesser price, only to watch two Japanese bidders face off across the arena from each other and go at it. The colt brought $240,000, and I walked away thankfully scratching my head.

‑‑ *Mixed sales are a good place to buy or sell.* Most buyers have a short list of horses that fit their order, and when they buy that one, they're done. This holds for all horse auctions, but at a mixed sale many times you can find an immature filly or one with a minor conformational fault that the pinhookers pass on. If they have a substantial enough pedigree, their potential as a breeding horse rather than as a racehorse can be far more significant – and potentially profitable.

Sales of two-year-olds in training are the last venue for those choosing to buy horses nearly ready to compete, and the consignors who bring them to market are some of the finest horsemen in the business. They use their skills to prepare young horses to put out their best effort for an eighth or a quarter of a mile, and some superior runners may come from these "breeze-ups." However, very few horses that work a furlong in less than 10 seconds make it at the races. They are used up getting to the sales and need a long period of recovery. This is true more so in North America than in Europe, where both racing and breeze-up sales are conducted on grass, a more forgiving surface, and the young horses hold up better to the stress of hard early training.

‑‑ *Value is relative.* The closer you get to a race the more it influences a horse's value. Weanlings are cheaper than yearlings, yearlings cheaper than two-year-olds in training. No horse is more overvalued than a three-year-old in the spring of the year before the classic races begin. A horse eligible for the Kentucky Derby has its greatest value the day before the race and may have considerably less the day after. Although most horsemen agree that gelding male horses is a sound practice for those not possessing a potential stallion's pedigree, since it allows them to "keep their mind on business," it does have a significant effect on value. Geldings are worth a fraction of what they can potentially earn, usually 25-50 percent, since that's the only way they can return anything on your purchase price. The day they take a bad step, their value goes close to zero.

-- *Demeanor counts.* Check out how a horse behaves at the sale, especially in their stall. Nervous horses at the sales are nervous at the track as well. They expend too much energy in their fretting, some turning into stall-walkers, weavers or cribbers, all bad habits that must be dealt with just to get a horse to train properly. You will discover that many good horses spend much of their time sleeping and conserve their energy for racing.

-- *Look for the whole package.* A good head and eye on a horse are indicators of good temperament. You will learn to spot those traits with experience. I have asked trainers over the years what they want in a horse and the consensus has always been "fast." The next thing they say is, "Give me a smart horse."

-- *Don't subscribe to myths.* Perfect conformation is not required to make a successful racehorse. A horse's balance, attitude, and way of moving should trump picture-perfect knees or ankles, as testified to by a trip to the walking ring before a Grade I race. As the legendary breeder John Madden liked to say, "They come in all shapes and sizes." You should endeavor to learn about good conformation. No savvy horseman will advise you to buy a horse that is back at the knee or has a suspicious tendon, and you should be able to identify those faults. And don't eliminate late foals from your list at yearling sales. Double classic winners Northern Dancer and Thunder Gulch were foaled the last week in May, and they both did okay.

-- *Auctions are about walking.* You will watch horses walk until they walk in your sleep. Watching for overstep – the hind foot reaching past the corresponding fore foot in a stride – is a good way of evaluating a horse's walk. And for the most part, if a horse can't walk well, they won't run well. Smoothness, fluid-ity, balance, and grace are what you're looking for.

-- *Horses are all about maintenance.* A clever horseman once commented that you could get them for free and still not make money if you weren't careful. They all eat the same oats, but some have the capability of winning races or producing valuable offspring, and others may prove to have no purpose in life other than to be a handsome paddock decoration or some child's pleasure horse.

And finally …

-- *Always buy quality horses, quality pedigrees, and sound individuals.* I know, I'm repeating myself. But it is of utmost importance that you do not delude yourself into thinking you can turn someone else's nightmare into your dream horse.

The idea is getting your horse into the right starting gate.

CHAPTER 5

THE GAME'S AFOOT

"Nobody with a nice two-year-old in the barn ever committed suicide."

~ *Woody Stephens, Hall of Fame trainer*

Horse owners are a diverse group, no matter how you look at them. There are no requirements or qualifications to join the club. You put up your money and take your chances. I have known hedge fund billionaires and guys who owned a carwash to face off in the walking ring before a race, each filled with trepidation as their horses headed for the starting gate.

The journey for most racehorse owners starts when they are racing fans, playing the ponies and enjoying the atmosphere of the racetrack. From there they might take the leap into ownership alone, or they might hook up with a group to claim or buy a horse, then another horse, then another, and another. It is not a guarantee – more a superstition based on experience – but they might even stumble upon what can only be described as beginner's luck, while basking in that first photo in the winner's circle, surrounded by friends and admirers – and their very own racehorse.

One of the first important lessons of ownership is being able to discern quality in the racehorse. Although all Thoroughbreds descend from one of three 18th century stallions – the Godolphin Barb, the Beyerly Turk, and the Darley Arabian – they all did not inherit the same genes.

Therein lies the reason we race them against each other: To find out which one is the fastest.

In order to tell the difference between real gold and fool's gold, between substance and flash, it is important to know what kind of races attract the horses with the most class and quality. The following categories define the various levels of com-petition, from top to bottom:

Stakes races – No matter their level of investment, every owner's ultimate aspiration is to win a stakes race because of the prestige attached and the handsome financial return. Most stakes races (short for sweepstakes) require the horse owner to put up eligibility fees. Those fees are added to a much larger contribution from the purse account managed by the track. The nomination fee, entry, and starting fees usually total only about 1.5 percent of the advertised purse.

There also is a type of stakes race known as an invitational, which is exactly what it sounds like. Owners are invited to run their horses in races of special status, without paying fees, but only if they meet certain levels of class and accomplishment. The $1 million Belmont Derby Invitational for elite three-year-olds, contested on the Belmont Park grass in July, is an example. By contrast, in 2019 it cost a minimum of $50,600 to nominate, enter, and start a horse in the Kentucky Derby for a shot at part of the $3 million purse.

Stakes races represent approximately four percent of races run in North America but pay out nearly 24 percent of all purse money. A racetrack management can define a stakes race in any manner it chooses, which is why you will find such events offering anything from a $5,000 stakes purse at small regional track to the multi-million-dollar purses of the Breeders' Cup Championships.

Stakes races have their own hierarchy, from the ultimate classics and world-famous events to lesser contests that serve as early proving grounds for up-and-coming horses. Graded stakes (called Group stakes outside the U.S. and Canada) are divided into three subcategories:

Grade/Group I – Classics and championship-quality races that represent the most important races in any country. They account for 0.1 percent of all races run.

Grade/Group II – Next in importance, these races represent 0.2 percent of all races.

Grade/Group III – These are of lesser stature but still stakes races worth winning, making up about 0.4 percent of all races.

There are also stakes races not labeled with a Grade or Group rating. These are generally referred to as "Listed" races, and sometimes they attract enough quality runners to be considered for elevation to Grade or Group status.

The Grade and Group designations provide the owner guidance, but only in broad strokes. Due to the differences of racing rules and conduct in various countries, it is a good idea to consult with an experienced advisor when attempting to evaluate the form anywhere beyond your own backyard. Some European countries have an extremely high percentage of Group races and run many of them with very short fields, a lack of depth that nevertheless imparts "black type" stakes status to the pedigrees of those horses and their relatives. In Ireland, for instance, where nearly 5 percent of all races hold Group status, it is common for the Coolmore consortium to have four or five horses in the same contest. As a result, less than superior runners can be accorded stakes horse status, when by comparison they might be nothing more than average racehorses in North America.

A similar theme applies to South American runners in Argentina, Venezuela, Brazil, Chile, and Peru, where a dearth of superior runners can inflate the form of mediocre horses who run up impressive scores in Group II and III stakes and occasionally even a Group I.

Consigned by Vinery Sales, Agent XLV

Barn		Hip No.
1 & 2 & 3	**Magic Happens**	1

Magic Happens
Dark Bay or
Brown Mare;
foaled 2016

	Awesome Patriot	Awesome Again	Deputy Minister
			Primal Force
		Tizamazing	Cee's Tizzy
			Cee's Song
	Hollybygolly (2003)	Old Trieste	A.P. Indy
			Lovlier Linda
		Stelluchella	Honor Grades
			Wandering Lace

By **AWESOME PATRIOT (2008)**. Black-type winner of $114,600, Alydar S.
(HOL, $43,020), etc. Sire of 5 crops, 5 black-type winners, $4,708,425,
including Cariblanco ($412,867, St. Leger [G1], etc.), Bella Sofia ($405,-
100, Longines Test S. [G1] (SAR, $275,000), etc.), El Animador ($72,-
485, Julio Castro Ruiz [G3], etc.), Awesome Arrow [L] ($105,560).

1st dam
HOLLYBYGOLLY, by Old Trieste. Unplaced in 2 starts. Dam of 5 other foals, 3
  winners, including--
  In the Dark (c. by Discreet Cat). 3 wins at 4, $111,526.
  Jackie Black (f. by Discreet Cat). 2 wins at 3, $37,178.

2nd dam
STELLUCHELLA, by Honor Grades. Winner at 4, $42,985. Dam of--
  EX EX EX (c. by Read the Footnotes). 7 wins, 3 to 7, $187,801, New York
  || Stallion Series S.-R (SAR, $60,000).
  Alfonsina (f. by Grand Slam). 2 wins at 2, $120,547, 2nd Valley Stream S.
  || **[G3]** (AQU, $21,430), Old Hat S. **[G3]** (GP, $20,000), 3rd Cicada S. **[G3]**
  || (AQU, $10,980). Producer.
  Inner Peace. Unraced. Dam of 3 foals, 2 winners, including--
    SNOWBALL (f. by Apriority). 6 wins, 3 to 5, 2021, $311,780, Louisiana
      Legends Soiree S.-R (EVD, $45,000), EVD Distaff S.-R (EVD, $36,000),
      Louisiana Legends Mademoiselle S.-R (EVD, $36,000), Louisiana Cup
      Filly and Mare Sprint S.-R (LAD, $30,000), 2nd Equine Sales Oaks-R
      (EVD, $15,000), Shantel Lanerie Memorial S.-R (FG, $15,000), Louisi-
      ana Legends Mademoiselle S.-R (EVD, $13,300), etc.

3rd dam
WANDERING LACE, by Private Account. Winner at 2, $5,415. Dam of--
  DRINA. 11 wins, 4 to 7, $205,682, Vizcaya H. [L] (CRC, $30,000), etc. Dam of
  || **SPAIN [G1]** ($3,540,542), **PUERTO BANUS [G2]** ($380,410, sire), **FAN-**
  || **TASTIC SPAIN [G3]** ($362,208), **PATH OF THUNDER** ($246,170, dam of
  || **EXCITED [G3]**, $244,796; etc.), **Saint Pierre** [L] (6 wins, Total: $140,979).
  Wandering Pine. Winner at 3, $24,180. Dam of **CAPOMORANO** (Clasico
  || Laffit Pincay [L], etc.). Granddam of **PLEASCACH [G1]** (Total: $814,401).
  Pretty Pretty Lady. 2 wins, $26,612. Dam of **Prime Realestate** ($145,901).
RACE RECORD: At 2, unplaced in 1 start; at 3, three wins, 3 times 2nd; at 4,
  unplaced in 1 start. Earned $25,714.
PRODUCE RECORD: 2021 no report.

The typical catalog page is filled with race ratings.

Of course, there have been notable exceptions. The most dramatic might be Canonero II, a crooked-legged colt who began his career with a mediocre record as a two-year-old in Venezuela. He even was sent briefly to California to test his early class, to no avail. However, when he returned to the U.S. in 1971 as a 3-year-old, he dominated the Kentucky Derby, even though he was considered a complete outsider. Canonero II would verify his ability by taking the Preakness, but he came up short in the Belmont Stakes due to a hoof ailment.

Canonero aside, the road to success in the horse business is best taken through a careful evaluation of stakes wins and placings, especially in Grade and Group races. That's where the value of a horse lies as a breeding animal, making it of utmost importance to verify that the stakes are of real quality.

Allowance races – Allowance races are the stepladder up which horses compete, based on their previous achievement. They will have such designations as "non-winners of two races" and "non-winners of a race other than maiden or claiming." The terms are somewhat self-explanatory, suggesting that at each step along the way, the competition will be more challenging. A horse who successfully negotiates the levels of allowance racing is most likely ready to dive into the world of stakes racing.

Horses entered in such races receive "allowances" in the weight they will carry, in the form of the jockey and saddle. Weight is added or subtracted from a baseline weight depending recent performance, age, time of year, and gender.

Claiming races – Claiming races form the bedrock of most of the programs run at North American racetracks. Horses running in claiming races have a price tag attached, and qualified owners can shop at will, according to certain rules and procedures.

The reasoning behind the claiming system is simple. For a variety of reasons, horses reach certain levels of competition.

When it is determined a horse is unable to compete in the higher quality range, movement into the claiming ranks is necessary for them to have an opportunity to win against horses of similar ability. Slower horses will never beat faster horses, but that does not mean they never have a chance of making any return on the owner's investment.

There also is the attraction of playing a game within the game. Owners with a claiming operation try to run their horses against inferior competition in an attempt to win a race and, in most cases, retain possession of the horse. Claiming represents a form of risk and reward with almost immediate gratification that can be very appealing to an investor.

It is unreasonable to think that a stakes horse might emerge from a claiming race, but there have been some notable exceptions that make for interesting history.

Charismatic, a husky chestnut with white stockings, started his career with eight losses, at which point he was entered twice for claiming prices of $62,500. Such an amount is hardly chump change, but if some adventurous owner had paid the price, they would have bought the eventual winner of the Kentucky Derby, Preakness, and the title as 1999 Horse of the Year. But no one did, which left all the glory to owner Robert Lewis and trainer Wayne Lukas, along with the task of explaining why they ever risked losing their champion in a claiming race in the first place.

"I'd be foolish to stand here and tell you I thought he was going to win this race," Lukas said after Charismatic won the Derby. "I probably never misjudged a horse so much early on as this one. But he just gets better and better every day."

In 2004, for a claiming price of $50,000, owner Steve Kenly landed a three-year-old gelding of modest ability who had a chance, they figured, of perhaps winning a minor stakes race at the L.A. County Fair. Unfortunately, Lava Man failed to make that dream come true. Instead, over the next four years under the care of trainer Doug O'Neill, Lava Man won every major race for older horses in California and racked up earnings of $5.2 million for Kenly and his partner, Jason Wood. In 2015, Lava Man was elected to the Thoroughbred racing Hall of Fame, joining such elite former claimers as John Henry, Stymie, and Seabiscuit.

All owners and trainers who claim horses are looking for bargains that they feel they can improve with their own methods. Sometimes this is only a matter of a change in the horse's diet, different shoeing, needed dental work, or a new training regimen. Most claims are considered successful if they can end up winning for a higher claiming price than the price for which they were taken in the first place. Then again, there may be another Charismatic out there, being risked in a claiming race, or a Lava Man just waiting for a new home.

Handicap races – These races are primarily found in European racing programs, fielding horses who would be in claiming races in North America. Horses are rated by handicap weights – rather than claiming dollar amounts – and usually race against their peers. If an owner wants to try and "steal" a win by facing lower-rated competition, his horse must carry heavier weight. Should an owner choose to jump up in class to try for a more lucrative purse against tougher company, the horse will carry less weight than the competition. In this manner, European handicaps do not encourage as much shuffling of horses among owners and trainers, as happens in the claiming game.

Horses of lesser ability in North America can also be found in races weighted by subjective handicaps. These are called *starter handicaps*, contests bringing together horses that have run for certain claiming price levels. Starter handicaps give owners a chance to run their claiming horses at their proven level without risk of losing them through a claim.

As noted, stakes races comprise only a small percentage of the total events run over a year's time. As your horse progresses in its racing career, it will find its level of competitiveness. Over time, only half the Thoroughbreds in any foal crop will make it to the races and only half of those will win a maiden event at any level. These are daunting statistics, but if you don't face reality before you start in the horse business, it's going to be way too late when you have to pay the feed bills.

Racehorse ownership has both its privileges and its responsibilities. Upon approaching the stable gate of any racetrack, one can expect to be stopped by a security guard and asked for a license or an identifying badge. Without such credentials you would be asked to wait while your trainer is contacted and sends someone to accompany you on a day pass. Each trainer is required to put his owners' names on a "badge list" which may be part of his stall application.

Every racing jurisdiction requires a Thoroughbred owner to apply for a license before their horse runs in a race. In the case of a new owner, you will be required to pay a fee and go through the application process, which includes fingerprinting and a photo. Once issued, your badge must be worn when inside the stable area, and in some jurisdictions, it will serve as an entry pass to the track as well.

Some tracks allow guests to accompany owners to the races, while others require that guests be put on a will call list for day passes. Most states require an owner to renew their license every year, although there are a few states that offer a three-year license. Many tracks have someone in the role of a concierge or horsemen's liaison who can help you with guest admittance, seats, and dining reservations. If not, the racing office secretary is the castle guard and the person you need to know for help with such details.

(The National Racing Compact is a centralized authority that facilitates the owner licensing process and can help an owner obtain a license in multiple racing jurisdictions. An application can be filled out online and details can be found in Appendix 2).

For the truly new to the sport, potential racehorse ownership should come with a knowledge of how racing is funded through betting. In 2020, the various legal methods of placing bets on horse racing in North America handled a total of $11.6 billion. Tracks earn their money through their commission, called the "takeout," a set percentage deducted from the betting pool of each race which they split with the horse owners via purses after paying taxes and other compulsory government fees.

Most of that $11.6 billion in 2020 bets was gambled at sites – online and otherwise – away from the racetracks. No matter where the betting is collected, however, the concept behind making those bets remains the same. Some tracks have their own programs for educating new fans in handicapping and betting. A potential horse owner can learn something through these programs applicable to your new business, and at the very least such seminars can be an entertaining way to mingle with members of the gambling public. Be prepared to encounter gregarious, self-appointed experts among the audiences, but for genuine expertise stick with listening to the people on the dais. Argue about the weather with the rest.

From soup to nuts, horse racing is a gamble, whether in breeding, owning, racing, buying, or selling. But no matter what your level of involvement, it is important to have a basic knowledge of handicapping and wagering strategy. An excellent starting point for anyone interested in learning the ropes is a book called *Betting on Horse Racing for Dummies*, by Richard Eng, who has been a racing writer and handicapper for the Las Vegas Review-Journal, a columnist for *Daily Racing*

Form, and the host of a horse racing radio program. He also was part of the ABC Sports team that covered the Triple Crown.

Betting on Horse Racing for Dummies is an easy-to-understand guide that helps new visitors to the track enjoy the sport and make smart bets. It explains what to look for in horses and jockeys, how to read a *Racing Form*, how to do simple handi-capping, and how to manage betting funds in order to make wagers that stand a good chance of paying off. It also makes for a smarter horse owner.

Learn how to read the *Daily Racing Form* as if it were the *Wall Street Journal*. Just as you wouldn't want your stock broker to buy random stocks for you, if you can't handicap a race, you will have no idea where to place your horses, and unrealistic expectations will quickly send you out the door.

Learn how to read a sales catalog. This is where all that glitters truly is not gold. Thoroughbred pedigrees have been compiled for over two centuries and contain priceless information ... if you know what you are looking at. If you do not, they might as well be written in Mandarin. Horsemen speak of "black-type" – the highlighted races won by horses in a pedigree – as if it were the key to the kingdom, but trust me, all black type not created equal. The bold face print looks good on the catalog page, but a stakes winner at Hastings Park in British Columbia is not of the same quality as one who earned that typeface at Belmont Park. Be aware that the people who put those catalogs together are in the horse selling business.

When it comes to understanding the actual world of racehorse ownership, however, that is where your *Thoroughbred Investors Bible* comes in, chapter and verse. You have purchased a horse or have been involved in its breeding. Now what?

Thoroughbreds go through a series of programs after they reach the fall of their yearling year that commence with the "breaking," or gentling, stage during which young horses are first introduced to the saddle and the weight of a rider on their backs. This is done at a farm or training center, and many times the future success or failure of an individual horse may depend on the skill of the person supervising the breaking process. Consider carefully who will break your horses and seek the best you can find in your area.

If a young horse has had its early preparation at a training center that is unfamiliar to your trainer, expect them to proceed cautiously when your two-year-old arrives at the track. Even if your trainer knows and respects those who handled the breaking process and a period of light galloping to get the fitness that is referred to as "bottom," you can anticipate your horses to have at least 45 days more galloping before they have their first breeze. After another 45 days, during which they are given carefully spaced, timed workouts, most two-year-olds are ready for their first race.

Even so, your expectations should be based on what you should already know to be your trainer's tendencies. Some trainers, including Todd Pletcher and Wesley Ward, like to have their young horses ready to win their first time out, while others – Bob Baffert and Aidan O'Brien come to mind – prefer to let the initial outing be an opportunity to gain some valuable racing experience. Both styles work and neither is better than the other, as evidenced by the multiple graded stakes wins accumulated by each of those trainers.

Except in rare instances, two-year-olds only run against other two-year-olds. Three-year-olds stay with their age group through the first part of the year, after which they must compete with older horses for most of the best purse opportunities. Two-year-olds can be compared to high school athletes, three-year-olds to college athletes, and Thoroughbreds four and older to professionals. Few younger human athletes are very competitive outside their peer groups, and neither are horses, although there are rare and fascinating exceptions.

In 1978, the French filly Sigy established herself as the best two-year-old of her gender in France, where she was trained by the remarkable Criquette Head. Knowing her filly well, Head tossed Sigy in against males of all ages in the Group 1 Prix de l'Abbaye, one of the premier races of the Parisian fall season. Among her opponents was three-year-old Solinus, the best sprinter in England and Ireland, but he was no match for Sigy, who led from the start of the 1,000 meters (about 5 furlongs) and won by three lengths.

Although it has become the custom in the U.S, for horses to compete against their own gender, this is not the norm in the rest of the world, where female horses regularly compete against males. Americans have grown accustomed to European trainers shipping female horses stateside for the Breeders' Cup events and beating the boys, beginning with Pebbles in the 1985 Turf and including Miesque, Ridgewood Pearl, Six Perfections, Miss Alleged, Goldikova, Found, and Enable. But American-trained mares also have had their share of Breeders' Cup success against males, led by Breeders' Cup Classic winner Zenyatta and including turf sprinter Mizdirection and the milers Royal Heroine, Tepin, and Uni.

Once your horse has been in training for those initial 90 days, you can expect the trainer to begin thinking about what type of maiden race they will best be suited for. Maidens are horses of either sex which have never won a race, and there are two basic categories. *Maiden special weight* is the equivalent of an allowance race for non-winners. All starters carry the same weight, only subject to an allowance for fillies running against males. *Maiden claiming* races attract horses that can be claimed for a specific price, e.g. $20,000, or for a price range, such as $20,000-$18,000. Weight allowance is made for a horse entered for the lower price, usually a pound or two per $1,000.

Obviously, horses considered to have allowance and stakes potential would not be entered in maiden claiming race. The previously mentioned Charismatic was an exception, or more dramatically there was Maximum Security, the three-year-old champion of 2019 who ran for a $16,000 claiming price in his first start as a two-year-old. The owners of those young "claimers" dodged a bullet and retained their colts.

The knowledgeable owner will come to understand that the racing plans for all horses are dictated by a publication called the *condition book*. Published periodically throughout extended race meets, the condition book offers a selection of daily races in a variety of categories, from stakes races to maiden claimers. The condition book is authored by the track's racing secretary, and at most tracks the books cover a period of 10-14 days. Over the course of a race meet, the types of races are spread out to recur at about three-week intervals

The races listed for most tracks follow a similar format to the following examples from a condition book for Monmouth Park in New Jersey. The particulars include the category of race, the total purse and any supplemental monies from state programs, age and/or sex restrictions, weight to be carried and conditions for weight allowances, and the distance and surface the race will be contested on:

First Race. The 1st running of the Presious Passion Stakes, $75,000. For three-year-olds and upward. No nomination fee; $250 to enter; $500 to start; $250 supplementary nominations may be made at time of entry. Weights: 3-year-olds, 119 lbs.; Older 124 lbs. The winner to receive $45,000; $15,000 to second; $7,500 to third; $4,000 to fourth; $2,000 to fifth; $1,500 sixth through last. Non-winners of a sweepstakes in 2019 allowed 3 lbs.; $40,000 twice since May 1, allowed 5 lbs.; $36,000 since June 1, allowed 7 lbs. (Maiden, claiming or state bred allowance races not considered). The winning owner to receive a trophy. Nominations Close Saturday, August 24, 2019. One mile and one-half (turf).

Second Race. Allowance. Purse $47,500 (plus 40% N.J.-bred enhancement). For three-year-olds and upward which have never won

a race other than maiden, claiming, starter or state-bred allowance, or which have never won two races. Three-year-olds 119 lbs. Older 124 lbs. Non-winners of a race since July 31 allowed 2 lbs. A race since June 30, 4 lbs. Races where entered for $30,000 or less not considered in allowances. Five and one-half furlongs (turf).

Fifth Race. Claiming. Purse $26,000 (plus 40% N.J.-bred enhancement). For fillies and mares, three years old and upward which have never won three races. Three-year-olds 119 lbs. Older 124 lbs. Non-winners of a race since June 30 allowed 3 lbs. Claiming price $20,000, For Each $1,000 To $18,000 1 lb. Races where entered for $16,000 or less not considered in allowances. One Mile.

Some tracks require the horse's foal certificate to be on file and base eligibility on the date they were received by the Horse Identifier's office. If your horse fits the conditions of the race and is ready to roll, entries are taken on a designated day from the time the racing office opens until a cutoff time. (The entry cutoff time is not written in stone and occasionally, if entries are light, the racing secretary will stay open for business late into the day.) At that point, the racing secretary will assemble the program of races, arranging them in whatever order fits the wagering menu.

A list of the races – including post positions and jockeys – is posted on a sheet referred to as an "overnight." The term is a throwback to the days when tracks took entries one day and ran the races the next. Nowadays, entries are taken anywhere from 48 to 96 hours ahead of the racing card to allow for last-minute changes and to afford horseplayers and public handicappers more time to do their homework. Traditionally, the overnight could be found at the track's racing office, but these days they are readily available on a variety of racing websites.

Even though tracks present anywhere from seven to twelve races on each program, a date in a condition book can offer upwards of fifteen possible races, since not all races will attract enough entrants to warrant being carded. When a race in the book does not "go" as advertised, this can be frustrating to both owners and trainers with a horse primed and ready to race. Racing secretaries must consider the economics of the business, though, and avoid carding too many races with only a handful of runners, fearing a late scratch that would negatively impact betting. The larger the field, the more bets are made, and the more is earned by both the racetrack and the purse fund. Except for certain circumstances, anything less than a field of eight is undesirable.

If a race falls just shy of attracting sufficient entries, the racing secretary is likely to offer the race again for the next day's program as an "extra" listed on the overnight sheet. On the flipside, there are those races that attract too many entrants, creating what is called an "also eligible list" of the horses not in the main body of the race. They do have the opportunity to run if there are any scratches. Otherwise, your horse is out of luck. You must wait until that kind of race is offered again or choose another type of race for your runner. Some tracks allow entries in turf races for horses that will run in the event of rain and the event is taken off the turf to be run on the main track and the horses that are strictly grass runners are allowed to scratch. These are called Main Track Only (MTO) entries and are worth considering if the forecast is iffy, as you may find yourself in an easier spot than against the original field. At most tracks, fields are generally restricted to 14, the maximum number of stalls in most starting gates, and some races on turf courses will be limited to even fewer because of safety concerns.

In short, if your horse needs to start in a six-furlong maiden special and does not make it into the field, expect that race to recur in two or three weeks. There's a good chance you'll get your chance then as horses that are excluded receive preference.

Prior to entry, trainers will consult with a jockey agent to gauge the availability of a specific rider. Jockeys receive 10 percent of what their mount earns for finishing first, 5 percent for second and third, and a flat fee ranging from $75 to $150 for any unplaced mount, depending on the standards of the jurisdiction. Jockey agents are allowed to represent two riders and traditionally receive 25-30 percent of each rider's income. Jockey fees are regulated by an agreement between the local horsemen's association and the Jockeys' Guild, while in many states the racing commission also has a say.

Some trainers, should they have a large enough stable, need their own rider they can rely on without having to constantly shop around. Such an arrangement is rarely committed to in writing, but the understanding is that the jockey gives a trainer and/or an owner "first call" on their services. This can be a mutually beneficial situation, especially if the stable is deep with quality runners, and if the rider is free to accept mounts from other stables as long as the first call trainer does not have a horse in the race.

It will come as no surprise to learn that there is a good deal of maneuvering and negotiating that goes on for mounts. Agents usually prefer to keep their options open to the last possible moment in order to keep their rider available for the main contenders.

Occasionally, there will arise a situation where agents will jump from one commitment to another. If you are the trainer or owner, this is referred to as being "spun." Should a jockey and agent try to renege on a confirmed call, the track stewards may require them to fulfill their original commitment or face fines and sanctions. Should an owner or trainer replace a jockey at the last minute without due cause, they may be required to pay both the new rider they engaged and the one they replaced.

A memorable instance of this was the case of Forever Unbridled in the 2017 Breeder's Cup Distaff at Del Mar. Her owner, Charles Fipke, had decided to make a jockey switch to John Velazquez at entry time after allegedly making a previous commitment to Joel Rosario, who had ridden Forever Unbridled in her previous start. Rosario's agent protested, since it was too late for him to find another mount for the $2 million race, and the track stewards ruled that the dual jockey fee rule would apply to whatever Forever Unbridled won in the race. She won, and Fipke was on the hook for $110,000 to both Velazquez and Rosario. But the owner protested the ruling, and, not surprisingly, the matter ended up in civil court.

The distribution of prize money is rarely that complicated. Nevertheless, a very important person in the owner's racing world is the Horsemen's Bookkeeper, who looks after the financial accounts of all owners. Their office is usually in the vicinity of the racing office, from where they credit purse earnings and claim proceeds, process stakes nomination fees, and disburse funds whenever requested by the owner. The Horsemen's Bookkeeper also distributes payment to the jockeys for their fees and to the pony riders taking horses to the gate. At most tracks, there is also an automatic donation from each winning purse for Thoroughbred retirement funds.

In addition to the daily fee charged per horse, your trainer will bill you directly for 10 percent of winning purses, unless a different deal has been established. In recent years, it has become customary for trainers to bill for an additional 2-3 percent to be paid the stable help on top of their wages. When all is said and done, owners can expect to net 75-80 percent of the horse's purse earnings.

In most states, the standard division of purses is 60 percent to the winner, 20 percent to second, 10 percent to third, and five percent to fourth. In recent years some venues have taken to stretching the payouts, lowering first money to 55 percent, and taking a point or two from the other placings to allow for paying back as far as fifth and sixth. Some tracks also have instituted purse shares for all starters, amounting to appearance fees that are small but welcomed.

Proceeds from horses claimed are available through the Horsemen's Bookkeeper. Race winnings are available to the owner as soon as the post-race drug test clears the state lab, usually within 72 hours. As part of the internal security system of the sport, post-race tests are designed to determine if any prohibited substances have been given to affect performance, or if any permitted medications have been given in excess of prescribed amounts. These tests are performed on several horses following every race, usually the winner and the second finisher plus a horse chosen at random. In some instances, a losing favorite also may be tested.

Beyond the sometimes tedious details of ownership, there are some fun perks, and one of them is deciding what to call your horse.

A horse's name is important. This might seem a frivolous notion, but consider that Secretariat, Whirlaway, War Admiral, Affirmed, and Zenyatta might have been treated differently around the barn if their names had been Dingbat, Dogface, Lazy Al, Plugfoot, or Ugly Sally.

The Jockey Club, established in 1894, oversees the naming and registration process and issues every horse's foal certificate. Thoroughbreds need to have a name request submitted by February 1 of their two-year-old year. After that, there is a modest late penalty.

The Jockey Club maintains an easily accessible current list of names already taken, or reserved, as well as a roster of unavailable names. These unavailable names fall into a number of categories, including past champions, Hall of Fame members, and the winners of such races as the Kentucky Derby, Preakness, and Belmont Stakes. In short, you may think you have the next Man 'o War, but you can't name him that.

In addition to the provisions of the published naming rules (see Appendix 3), the Registrar of The Jockey Club reserves the right of approval on all name requests, setting themselves up as the arbiter of good taste. Still, there remains plenty of room for creativity, and owners become well known for the inventive ways in which they name their horses.

Owners also get to design their own set of racing colors, to be displayed on the jersey and cap of the jockeys who ride their horses. This is no minor responsibility. The colors flown by famous horses become automatically iconic, and many of them are imprinted on the memories of racing fans, just as the flags of certain nations are universally familiar.

In New York, The Jockey Club maintains a strict set of guidelines when it comes to the design of racing colors. The requirements date back more than a century and are so strict as to be amusing. Outside of New York, however, The Jockey Club has no jurisdiction in terms of racing colors, and they can run the gamut from soberly conservative to wild and crazy. A warning, however. Even if an owner does not plan on competing in New York on a regular basis, there is always a chance that someday they might have a horse worthy of running in a race at Saratoga or Belmont Park. When it comes to the design of racing colors, it is not a bad idea to at least consult the rules of The Jockey Club, because The Jockey Club will not let you run under colors that stray significantly from their restrictions (see Appendix 4).

One last piece of advice on silks design. Without high-powered binoculars, no matter where you race you probably will not be able to see your unique logo or lettering emblazoned on your colors as the horses run down the distant backstretch. But you can follow your horse if its jockey is wearing bright hues that stand out in a crowd. When it came to designing silks for my Star Stable, I chose a red body with a yellow star, front and back, yellow stripes down the sleeves, and yellow star on a red cap. Believe me, I always knew where my horse was.

Trainer D. Wayne Lukas with champion colt Charismatic

CHAPTER 6

THE TRAINING GAME

"I like to keep myself in the best company and my horses in the worst."

~ *Horatio Luro, trainer of Northern Dancer*

Should your intentions be specifically racing oriented, or if you intend to use racing as a jumping off point before getting into breeding, it is strongly recommended that you spend at least a week or two becoming acquainted with racetrack life. A basic understanding of what goes on at the track will serve you well. Indeed, you will find there are few places more enchanting and relaxing than a racetrack barn at dawn.

Once inside the stable gates of any racetrack, you will behold row after row of racehorse barns, identical except for the numbers at the roofline and the logos of individual trainers. Inside the cover of the barn, known as the "shedrow," there will be wall plaques bearing the name or insignia of the trainer alongside identifying nameplates for each horse. If you see an "NPZ" monogram you are in the barn of two-time Derby winner Nick Zito. A simple white diamond on a green field is all you need to know that you are in the house of Hall of Famer Bill Mott. "DWL" can only be Wayne Lukas, "TAP" signifies multiple national champ Todd Pletcher, and Steve Asmussen, trainer of Hall of Fame horses Curlin and Rachel Alexandra, favors a stylized "A" in a rustic frame.

The same trainer logo can be found on the saddle towels as the horses go to the track for morning exercise. In addition to their advertising properties, the towels provide official clockers with a way of identifying horses in their workouts.

Daily activities begin well before dawn as grooms check their horses and take temperatures. In preparing for morning exercise, grooms will consult the "set list" usually posted outside the door of the trainer's office. The regimen might consist of a gallop of anywhere from 1 1/2 to 2 miles, or a timed workout at a pace of the trainer's choosing.

Observe as the groom gives his horse a thorough brushing before adding the saddle and bridle, protective "polo" bandages on each lower leg, and perhaps even "run down" patches on the heels to prevent rubbing the hair and skin when running over a coarse, sandy surface. Bandages and patches are then covered with a second layer of Vet Wrap, and the horse is ready to go, although some with a tendency to nick their hooves may also wear protective rubber ankle cuffs, called "bell boots." Their shape explains their name.

Each groom cares for three to five horses. Their responsibilities include washing, currying, feeding, and stall cleaning, as well as being the trainer's first line of information regarding any change in a horse's behavior or physical condition. The barn also employs hotwalkers who will handle the horses after exercise while they cool down and assist the grooms in the bathing routine. Generally speaking, a horse will walk for about half an hour after morning exercise, having either jogged, galloped or breezed, or perhaps had riderless exercise in the company of a horse and rider, referred to as "ponying."

In its essence, training horses is a simple task made complicated by the demands of a sport riddled with countless variables. John Tammaro, Jr., the trainer of North American champion two-year-old Deputy Minister and five Canadian champions, said it best: "We're all doing the same thing, different."

Before the advent of the computer and personal data files, every trainer's desk was home to a daily training chart recorded on a graph-like calendar often provided gratis by feed or tack companies. To this day, most trainers still use the old-school chart to plot each horse's daily exercise. In the spirit of "doing the same thing different," each trainer follows a specific pattern customized to individual horses.

I highly recommend acquiring – and reading! – the classic racetrack primer *Training Thoroughbreds*, written by Preston Burch. *Training Thoroughbreds* was published in 1953 and remains the definitive work on the subject. Three generations of Burches are in the racing Hall of Fame, including Preston's father, W.P. Burch, and his son, Elliott. Preston Burch distilled his experiences from a career of more than 70 years to offer invaluable insights into the development of a racehorse.

Darrell Wayne Lukas came to the Thoroughbred game after previous success in teaching, coaching, and a career training Quarter Horses to 24 world championships. Between 1980 and 2013, Lukas won four Kentucky Derbies, six runnings of the Preakness, and four renewals of the Belmont Stakes. "D. Wayne," as he became known, received the Eclipse Award as Outstanding Trainer four times, and trained 20 winners of Breeders' Cup races. In 1999, Lukas was inducted into the Thoroughbred Racing Hall of Fame.

Upon receiving the John W. Galbreath Award in 1998 for outstanding entrepreneurship in the equine industry, Lukas mused on traditional behaviors of the racehorse trainer:

"Where do trainers get off thinking that a guy who comes in, buys a yearling for fifty-thousand dollars, or a quarter-million or whatever his level is, should have to ask the trainer's permission to see it?" Lukas said. "That's how this game has been for a hundred years. The owners have to call up to hear their trainers say, 'No, you can't come to the barn today, you're not allowed.' I think that's crazy. All the people I've had success with are people I pulled in and got involved."

This is precisely the attitude you're looking for in both your advisor and your trainer. The Lukas legacy testifies to the success of his methods as carried on by such proteges as Todd Pletcher, Kiaran McLaughlin, Dallas Stewart, Mike Maker, Randy Bradshaw, and Mark Hennig. All of them went on to admirable training careers after serving as assistants to Lukas.

There is a tacit agreement between racetracks and trainers that includes two main premises. First, the tracks will provide stabling in the form of stalls and use of the track to the trainers for an agreed number of horses. Second, the trainers are obligated to run those horses in races to be run at that track. Track officials take the trainer's participation level in account when allocating stalls, and with the exception of stakes horses that sometimes need to travel to compete in specific events, shipping out to run in race at another track identical to a race offered at one's home track is frowned upon.

Historically, trainers were restricted on the maximum amount of horses they could bring to the track based on the number of stalls in any one barn. At most tracks, barns hold anywhere between twenty and forty stalls, depending on their configuration. Also included in the barn are rooms for multiple uses. Trainers will convert one room to an office, another for storage of tack, feed, and other equipment, and others as needed for bare bones living quarters for stable personnel.

It once was a hard and fast rule that even Hall of Fame trainers like Woody Stephens, "Sunny Jim" Fitzsimmons, Max Hirsch, Mack Miller, Preston Burch, Hirsch Jacobs, and Ben and Jimmy Jones were allowed to fill a barn of up to 40 horses, but no more. However, in the mid-1990s, New York racing officials began granting permission to some trainers with access to large horse inventories to occupy a second or even a third barn, either on the track's grounds or at another track in the NYRA system. This included Aqueduct, located near JFK International Airport, and Saratoga in upstate New York, from which trainers can van horses back and forth to Belmont Park.

This single move of expansion, as innocently practical as it may have seemed at the time, led to the development of the modern "super trainer," defined as having more than 100 horses under their control. Such a trend fit well with the American way of "bigger is better," although there developed at least one negative effect. Trainers with such super-sized stables realized it was counter-productive to run more than one of their horses in a race, thereby shrinking the number of runners available to the racing program. As far as the trainer was concerned, though, he was not willing to risk the chance of upsetting one owner by beating him with a horse owed by another owner in the barn. At the very least, the losing owner had a right to question the pecking order in the stable.

A new owner must weigh the pros and cons when to comes to getting involved with a trainer of a large stables versus a smaller barn. You may want to throw your support to an up-and-coming trainer of growing local repute. Or your comfort zone might lean toward the big-name trainer who has classic race experience and a huge resume of stakes wins. In all cases, your intentions are paramount. The trainer you choose – large stable or small – will in the end be determined by your decision to attack the claiming game, buy yearlings or two-year olds in training, or breed your own runners for the racetrack.

Another innocent change had a huge impact on the training game. At one point the *Daily Racing Form*, in an effort to better serve its betting customers, began to publish trainer and jockey win percentages in the past performance charts. It may have helped the gamblers to some extent, but it certainly

Thoroughbred racehorses are pampered like royalty.

did not help those trainers who for whatever reason failed to achieve comparably high win rates. No one wanted to appear to be an underachiever, and so horses were withheld from maiden races until the ideal spot came up. Field sizes predictably shrank, and trainers with smaller stables lost horses to the super trainers, many even leaving the game for economic reasons.

Over a long period of time, it has been shown that the average winning percentage for a professional horse trainer who starts more than 100 runners per year would be in the range of 15-20 percent. The number may vary with the normal peaks and valleys of dealing with living creatures, and when you see a trainer spike upwards to 40 percent or dip to 10 percent, there almost always will be a period of adjustment during the year and they will finish in that 15-20 percent range.

However, when owners evaluate trainer simply based on a snapshot of win percentage statistics, there can be a dramatic shift away from some stables toward others, upsetting the equilibrium of the training environment as if all the passengers moved to the same side of the boat.

Please keep in mind that your personal expectations of winning should include a strong dose of reality. Reasonable success in racing is defined by winning one of every five starts. Anyone who surpasses the 20 percent winning rate over any significant period should thank their lucky stars – and brace for the inevitable return to a more realistic world.

The key, therefore, is to make that one win in five count for a lot, and hope that the other four run well enough to at least earn part of the purse. Racing, fortunately, is not a zero sum, winner-take-all endeavor. Second place can provide a pretty nice prize, and third through fifth can pay for a lot of feed bills.

No matter what, remember that patience, even in the face of a losing streak, is a priceless commodity. When I ran the Due Process Stables, one of our main focal points was the Saratoga meet. My boss, Robert Brennan, had a special affection for the town of Saratoga Springs and the century old racetrack, and for several years he rented a home on Union Avenue before buying a mansion on upper Broadway. In honor of the move, he named one of our colts Bye Union Ave.

Alas, the stable did not have much luck at the marquee Saratoga meet. After a few years of being shut out from the winner's circle, I began to dread the annual kickoff dinner Brennan hosted for several dozen of his friends. At some point in the table conversation, he would turn to me and ask, "Think we'll win a race this year?" To which I would reply with feigned confidence, "Definitely. This is our year."

We went seven years without a win at the Spa until I figured it out that we were consistently running over our heads, failing to heed Horatio Luro's advice about the company our horses should keep. We were running second and third in prestigious races like the Saratoga Special, the Whitney, and the Schuylerville, but second and third don't get your picture taken. And to an owner, valued by weight, a winner's circle picture is more precious than gold.

Brennan's patience finally was rewarded on Aug. 20, 1989, when big gray gelding named Yucca, trained by Phil Gleaves and ridden by Hall of Famer Angel Cordero, won a $30,000 claiming race on the Saratoga turf and took us to the winner's circle. Whew! Talk about a long time between drinks. We went on to score multiple wins every season thereafter, including a dream meet in 1993 when our homebred colt Dehere won all three of Saratoga's two-year-old stakes – the Sanford, the Saratoga Special, and the Hopeful – on his way to becoming an Eclipse Award-winning champion and the early favorite for the 1994 Kentucky Derby.

When the Due Process operation was in full swing, we had as many as five trainers handling our runners in different jurisdictions, mainly because we had so many homebreds and they needed to race where they could meet suitable competition or participate in state-bred restricted races. They needed to be winners in order to improve the pedigrees of our broodmares.

Paramount to achieving your goal of picking the right trainer is finding one who will tell you what you need to know, not what you want to hear. It is not easy to learn that the expensive racehorse you purchased has been injured or has no talent, but at some point, cutting losses must be part of a successful business plan, and feeding horses that cannot be competitive is the prime reason for those losses. The sooner your trainer can tell you that a horse is just not making the grade, the better off you are.

My personal preference for a trainer is for someone who has been an assistant in a large stable trainer or has worked for a highly reputable older trainer who perhaps handled only a limited number of well-chosen horses. Not only assistants, either, for sometimes the sons and daughters of such trainers learn their lessons well and go on to successful careers.

Once you have narrowed the process down to a few candidates, visit those trainers at work in the morning and watch their horses run in the afternoon. You will find that most trainers try to breeze their horses on Saturday mornings so that busy owners can be present. A few Saturday mornings spent in the clocking stands observing the training process will go a long way toward furthering your Thoroughbred education. And, since horses simply walk the day after a workout, you will note that the Sunday barn crew gets an easier day.

The best source for opinions on trainers likely would be the racing secretary at your local track. They would be able to give you their impression of a number of candidates, including personality traits and how they handle their business.

In general, trainers with a smaller stable will have more time to spend with clients. In contrast, the larger organizations are layered with assistants and secretaries that stand between you and the head trainer. They are expected to field your calls and take care of your needs, leaving the boss time to manage the horses.

Obviously, the amount of the capital you are expecting to invest will have some bearing on your trainer selection. Starting small with claimers or modestly priced yearlings, you will not be a candidate for the services of a trainer like Todd Pletcher, Bob Baffert, Chad Brown, or Steve Asmussen. Their business models cater to the owners with the deepest pockets, who spend their money on sales-topping stock. Other leading trainers may seem more accessible, but you should be aware that they may have arrangements to train almost exclusively for long term clients, like Shug McGaughey for the Phipps family of New York, or John Sadler for the Hronis Racing

Stable family of California's Central Valley. Some trainers of large stables, like Kelly Breen, Christophe Clement, or Graham Motion might have a contract with a principal patron that allows them to take horses from other clients as well. There also is the very real issue of a trainer simply having enough room in his racetrack stable for the horses of a new owner. They are only assigned so many stalls.

The history of racing is filled with stories of long-term relationships between owners and their trainers, and with just as many tales of owners who change their trainers as often as they change their socks. The delicate balance can be disrupted by a losing streak or a rash of minor injuries, with a result that an extended honeymoon can soon turn into an acrimonious divorce.

Such variables make the selection process of a trainer even more important, harkening back to the old adage, "Marry in haste, repent at leisure." If you are someone who needs an instant call-back or extra hand-holding, make sure you try to align your temperament with a trainer who appreciates you as much as you do him or her. There are certain thoughts to keep in mind:

-- *Choose a trainer who will communicate.* If they don't have time for your phone calls, perhaps they're not for you. Trainers like Pletcher, Baffert, and Ireland's Aidan O'Brien all agree that the line of communication between patron and trainer is an integral part of the relationship. A smart trainer will allocate several hours of each day to personal contacts, as well as employ someone to make sure the owner gets timely updates on any workouts or race entries. Many have their own interactive websites and will keep you apprised of your horse's progress with videos.

-- *Request regular reports from your trainer and advisor.* If they don't have time to do so, find people who will. Those who conduct their business correctly will have no problem providing invoices, bills of sale, and their own business plan, which in turn is part of yours. In many cases, it can be advantageous to be in a partnership with your trainer and advisor. This "skin in the game" concept works well if you write it down, remembering that oral contracts are only worth the paper they're printed on. And in no case should you authorize a trainer or agent to withdraw funds from your account with the Horseman's Bookkeeper. Best to open a line of communication yourself with the Horseman's Bookkeeper early on and they will respond to any requests you have for information or dispersal of your funds.

-- *Know your costs up front as much as possible.* The trainer's day rate and the veterinarian charges are the major expenses in any racing operation. In 1978, a $25 per horse/per day training rate was considered pricey. By 1984, it was the low end of the spectrum, available only at the second or third tier racetracks, and by 2020, top trainers like Pletcher, Brown, Baffert, Sadler, and Asmussen all commanded day rates well in excess of $100. Some of the increase could be attributed to rising costs of feed, bedding, tack, and transportation, although most of it would be a direct result of the cost of labor, workmen's compensation insurance, and state and local taxes.

Some trainers will offer to train on a "deal," charging little or no training fees in lieu of a higher than normal percentage of purse earnings, usually up to 50 percent instead of their usual 10 percent. This type of scheme may work at third-tier tracks where expenses are low and horses hard to come by, but in most cases, it is a poor deal for the owner. If you can't afford to pay daily fees, you certainly should question whether you can afford to be in the game at all. Plenty of trainers who make such deals end up getting burned when the undercapitalized owner decides the horse is not worth what they owe and elects to default on their agreement. The trainer is stuck with a horse he still must feed and care for even if it has no earning potential.

Often in partnerships, when decisions must be made by more than one interested party, the time-tested adage of the business applies: "Nothing comes between friends better than a good horse." When horses are slow, have physical problems, or no particular talent, your partner or partners will suffer with you, and the partnership could be strained. When your horse begins to win and shows promise, expect a horde of "experts" to emerge from the woodwork to give you free advice and cause undue pressure on partner decisions. However, if you and your partners have selected the right trainer and advisor, you will be able to tune out such distractions and share all aspects of the racing experience together.

In 2014, the Thoroughbred Breeders and Owners Association conducted a detailed survey with more than 270 Thoroughbred owners from around the U.S. inquiring about the cost of maintaining a racehorse over the period of a year. A summary of the results of that survey are reflected here:

Veterinary fees are dependent upon your trainer's habits and the health of your horse. Be sure you have a candid discussion with your trainer to learn about their philosophy concerning the extent to which a vet is going to be used on a normal day-to-day basis. A trainer who can be described as aggressive in their use of veterinary services can be expected to bill more than $700 per month/per horse. Moderate vet use will cost in the $300-$600 range, while occasional vet services will run less than $300.

Other expenses not included in the trainer's day rate include:

--*Farrier fees.* Racehorses are shod and re-shod every two to four weeks.

--*Vanning.* Many times your horse may ship to another track to race. Vanning charges depending on how far the horse is shipped and the difference in carriers.

--*Trainer travel costs.* When your horse ships to another track, your trainer must go along. Often, trainers will charge their owners for travel costs including mileage, hotel, and possibly airline tickets.

--*Feed Supplements.* There is a wide variety of feed supplements used by trainers to improve horse health and aid in training routine.

--*Race-day charges.* The day your horse races can involve charges such as bandages, run-down patches, the groom to lead your horse to the paddock and post-race cooling out, and a lead pony and rider to take your horse to the starting gate.

--*Percent of earnings.* Most trainers charge an owner 10 percent of the race earnings from each start where a horse earns a check, and some add on 2-3 percent for the stable help.

Now for a word about claiming. Certain trainers keep close track of the available inventory of claiming horses at a particular racetrack, and if you are a new owner intent on playing the claiming game, you will want to associate yourself with a person who knows the lay of the land. It will help, though, if you also know as much as possible about the nuts and bolts of claiming before wandering into the deep end.

Generally speaking, the claiming procedure is similar at all tracks. The owner puts money on account with the Horsemen's Bookkeeper and authorizes an individual trainer to submit any claims. Horses in claiming races run with a set price attached, and the successful claimant becomes the new owner immediately upon the race having been run, with a few exceptions that will be discussed later.

To claim a horse, a "claim slip" is filled out, placed in a sealed envelope, time stamped, and dropped in a locked claim box in the racing secretary's office. The claim slip includes the date, name of the horse to be claimed, the purchase amount, and the signature of the person authorized to claim on the owner's behalf. After the deadline, usually 15 minutes to post time, the box is unlocked and the claims are delivered to the stewards, who open and verify that they are filled out properly, with spelling and date correct. The stewards' office will verify sufficient funds are in the claimant's account and that the owner is properly licensed. If not, the claim will be voided.

When more than one claim is entered for any horse, the claims clerk will conduct a draw of lots using numbered balls or "pills" placed in a leather bottle. The number of pills corresponds to the number of claims made for a particular horse. For obvious reasons, this process is called a "shake," after which one pill is removed, indicating the winning claimant. Shakes are common for consistent claiming horses, and many claims are for females that have potential as broodmares. You and your trainer also might discover a horse who was an expensive auction purchase now entered for a claiming price that is a fraction of his original cost. The claim box can be stuffed with a dozen or more slips.

Once the claimant has been determined and all else is in order, the claims clerk will give the new trainer a delivery slip, after which the trainer or his assistant will go to the unsaddling area near the winner's circle or to the test barn and complete the physical transfer of ownership.

The best prospect for a claim is usually an older horse that has showed class and heart over a number of starts. Often these are geldings which have overcome a number of infirmities such as sore ankles or knees, enlarged tendons or suspensory ligaments, or ouchy feet, but they still show a will to win. Trainers who specialize in dealing with these infirmities are willing to take the chance they can find the key to moving such horses up the claiming ladder or even into stakes competition.

Depending on the venue, the value of claiming prices can run the gamut. They range from $5,000 price tags in maiden events to $100,000 for horses who otherwise might be found in allowance competition or minor stakes. There even have been claiming races for as high as $250,000 at top tier tracks, although they are more a novelty than a common practice.

For many years claiming was the ultimate roll of the dice, as the claimant was deemed to own the horse in question as soon as the starting gate opened. It didn't matter if the horse won the race, ran last, or dropped dead. Claim slip in, you own it. Claims could only be voided by the track stewards for financial discrepancies or deficiencies on the claim slip. In recent years, however, tracks have gone to an alternate method by which a horse that fails to finish, is pulled up lame, or is of questionable soundness following a post-race exam can be returned to the original owner and the transaction voided.

The claiming process is often referred to as a game within the game of racing, complete with a set of rules that are fairly consistent from state to state. Most states restrict how claiming horses can be entered again after they are claimed, known as being "in jail." The newly claimed horse, if entered within 30 days after the claim, must be entered for a minimum claiming price 25 percent higher than the recent claim price. This prevents the person who claimed the horse from dropping it in price – and therefore competition level – in order to cash a bet or quickly get rid of a bad investment. This rule varies slightly from state to state, so always check the specific rules with the racing secretary wherever you intend to compete with claimers. In some jurisdictions, there may be no "jail" time, or there might be rules that allow for horses that have taken time off to race "protected," or unable to be claimed in their first start back.

The risk in claiming horses is obvious. Not all horses are created equal, and many who break their maiden may place or win another race before steadily descending the claiming ranks, requiring weaker competition to be economically viable. Many of these horses have lost the will to win and never run well again, victims of minor infirmities. As an investor, you must deal with the unpredictable reality of buying a horse who has been in the care of someone now willing to give up the horse, for a price, but for an unknown reason. Full disclosure of a claiming horse's veterinary history has become a goal in several racing juris-dictions. But even if that becomes a reality, the evaluation of astute trainer is a necessity.

There are several things to keep in mind when contemplating the claiming route, notably that the younger horses tend to be overpriced based on the perception that they have more untapped potential. Neither do young horses have the niggling ailments that discourage them from running. As a result, they will run their truest races early, showing their ability level which can be measured and compared in terms of time and speed ratings.

Still, while they might look good on paper, pretty is as pretty does. Do not be lulled into thinking the trainer who dropped a horse in for a claiming price is a fool, while your trainer is a genius who will turn a bargain claim into a Derby horse. There is, however, something exciting about the acquisition of a horse that was desired by others. At the racetrack, claiming is the ultimate gamble, and the thrill of owning a horse who can give you instant action cannot compare with the long-term patience required in the purchase of a yearling, or the breeding of a stallion and a mare.

Seattle Slew immortalized at Hill 'n' Dale farm in Kentucky.

CHAPTER 7

WHERE THE GAME BEGINS

"My experience has taught me that a good horse, like a good gamecock, has no bad color. As to size, many big turnips are hollow."

~ *John E. Madden*

For its first century and a quarter, the United States was a largely agrarian society. City growth was tied securely to farm production. Post 1900, however, the urbanization of America took over, and farms began to consolidate or disappear, as vast portions of American industry became an investment source for foreign money.

At one point, the introduction of the automobile succeeded in removing horses from much of daily American life. Roads became better and more accessible, and travel by horse or horse-drawn carriage disappeared entirely. Most Americans in the 2020s will find their only exposure to animals, other than cats or dogs, takes place at a city zoo or a shopping center petting zoo. Today's kids consider horses an oddity and can only imagine them as a large version of their family pet, or a fantasy creature of an animated world.

Even a visit to a modern Thoroughbred farm is a far cry from that of a hundred years before. Of course, there remains the intrinsic beauty of a pastoral setting and the majesty of the

113

horses. If you can be present at a breeding farm in the winter or spring during the foaling season, you may have the opportunity to watch the birth of a colt or filly, an unforgettable experience. Otherwise, one can't help but be amazed by the complex nature of how the business has evolved.

As the source for all Thoroughbreds, the breeding farm is the bedrock of the industry. Close to one-third of all yearlings go to public auction, many of them having changed hands previously as weanling pinhooks, and many will be resold again as two-year-olds in training. While some have been raised at smaller family operations, plenty receive their early schooling at large commercial farms. They're all getting the same basic training, whether intended for resale or being retained for the breeder's racing stable.

While the costs of owning a racehorse have risen dramatically over the past few decades, in most jurisdictions and with few exceptions, purses have not kept pace with the costs of purchase and training, thus enhancing the desirability of breeding, either for resale or racing.

When it comes to setting up a breeding program, do not be the kind of Thoroughbred investor who listens to archaic notions and old wives tales. Be careful not to get too smart, too soon. You will get plenty of advice from those who have "been there and done that," and it might take you a few years of hard study to acquire enough independent knowledge to intelligently breed a good horse. Do not ignore modern data and breeding practices but do surround yourself with people who have added to their experience with up-to-date infor-mation and technologies. No single approach – be it heart measure-ment, gait analysis or computer program – offers the keys to the kingdom, but they all have value in certain situations. (Review Chapter 4 regarding the importance of a pedigree expert on your team.)

Every state with a breeding program will have a breeders association. They are happy to provide you with their roster of farms, and you should visit several to see the differences in how they operate. Because the breaking and training of young horses is so integral to the process of developing a commercial race-horse, your choice of farms likely will depend on the relation-ship your advisor or your trainer has with the facility. In the case of breeding farms, the importance of the skill and experience of the pre-natal and birthing crew cannot be underestimated, and first-hand knowledge of the farm's reputation is important. Kentucky has a number of organized farm tours which will provide a sense for how sophisticated the modern Thorough-bred operations have become. (Check with individual farms or go to the websites included in Appendix 7.)

If possible, ask if you can spend some time with the farm veterinarian as they make their rounds. These usually include examining newborn foals and palpating mares to determine if they are near ovulation. Also, during the breeding season you should arrange a visit to a stud farm to watch a breeding. Unlike other breeds of horses which may use artificial insemination, Thoroughbreds are required by The Jockey Club rules to inseminate by natural cover, which means they must complete the physical act. In the case of two large animals, this can be another unforgettable experience.

As noted earlier, the disparity between the cost of a horse in training and the possibility of a return on that investment from purse earnings paints a daunting picture. However, the more contemporary trend of a decrease in the foal crops compared to the number of races/total purses means your program has an improved chance to break even. You might even make money with a better than average horse, while attempting to increase the post-racing value of that horse along the way. The science of breeding is certainly not surefire, but with the right mare and the right stallion, and the right amount

A mare and her foal contemplate the future.

of luck, you have the chance to produce a valuable animal worth two-to-three times your investment.

Aphorisms abound in horse racing, many so charming that they beg to be repeated, whether true or not. Oldtimers will tell you to look for stallions that "stamp their get," meaning that their offspring will resemble them physically. This is a nice notion, but one need only look to studs like Bold Ruler, a stunning, nearly black horse whose most notable son was the flashy chestnut Secretariat, or Nijinsky II, a staunch bay that produced the superior chestnut runners Ferdinand, Sharastani, and Sky Classic.

More salient are the ruminations of the master horsemen. Some of my favorites are those delivered by John E. Madden, the legendary breeder and trainer known as the "Wizard of the Turf," who produced six Kentucky Derby winners: Old Rosebud (1914), Sir Barton (1919), Paul Jones (1920), Zev (1923), Flying Ebony (1925), and Plaudit (1898), which he also trained. His wisdom regarding the racing Thoroughbred is timeless:

"A good horse is dangerous in anybody's hands," Madden said. "It matters not who trains him if he has good qualities, for he is bound to show them sooner or later. If you were to ask me what makes a trainer or a jockey, I could reply quickly that they are made by good racehorses."

And as to breeding:

"A stallion is 75 percent of the stud" Madden said. "The mare contributes the vitality. Her control of form is slight. If you have any doubt in regard to this, take the result when a mare is mated with a jack. It always is a mule. The only change is color and size. Race mares rarely produce great performers. Their daughters seldom fail when properly mated."

On Madden's point, when buying a mare, look at her previous foals if possible. If there are faults are found that would prevent the foal from making a racehorse, you can expect the mare to pass on the same to her future babies. Likewise, the same qualities that make a superior racehorse, when passed on through the female line, will at some point repeat within a generation or two, even though the black type past the first dam might be meaningless to buyers reading a sales catalog. The combination of quality sire and the daughter of a superior racemare can be the key to your success. Such mares that consistently produce superior runners are referred to as "blue hens," a name derived from an exceptionally strong strain of fighting gamecock.

As you venture onto a quality Thoroughbred farm, several things will impress you immediately. It is hard to imagine a display of nature more sublime than the beauty of the mares and foals, secure in their wood-fenced fields, grazing peacefully or playing in the sun. Elsewhere on the farm, the luxurious life of a Thoroughbred stallion leaves little to be desired. They sleep in temperature controlled, oversized stalls filled with the finest straw, dine on a customized diet, and romp in their individual paddocks.

Make no mistake, though, such elegant simplicity comes at a price, calling for considerable effort and expertise from a dedicated group of unique individuals who work seven days a week for 52 weeks a year, foregoing the usual holidays and seasonal breaks in the service of the Thoroughbreds in their care.

As far as basic breeding expenses are concerned, farm board rates in the U.S. for a broodmare, either pregnant or "open," can vary from state to state but usually are $30 to $45 per day, plus additional expenses of monthly veterinary exams, farrier, tack, and supplements. After foaling, there is a small charge for the foal (a suckling) by the mare's side, ranging from $6 to $12, until the foal is weaned at six months. After that, the full board rate will apply.

In Europe the boarding rates are in the 20 to 45 Euro range. European breeders also must pay Value Added Tax (VAT) of anywhere from 6-12 percent on their bills, which makes the U.S. rates look like a bargain by comparison.

There are terms you will hear from the moment you wade into the breeding world (see the Glossary for an extensive vocabulary lesson). Commercial breeding farms that maintain stud horses are called as "stallion stations." The contract/appointment between mare owner and stallion owner is called a "booking," and the total of a stallion's appointments is his "book" of mares. Stallion stations usually do not board mares – normally a function of the smaller farms nearby – and the mares will ship in on the day of their breeding appointment with the stallion. In a well-run operation, the mare's conjugal visit may last less than half an hour from the time she gets off the van until she is on her way home.

In recent years, large stallion books often topped 150 breedings, with some stallions required to perform twice or even three times a day. Some nearly double their output by doing Southern Hemisphere duty at farms in Australia or

South America. In 2020, The Jockey Club adopted a rule limiting the annual breeding of individual stallions to a total of 140 mares in a calendar year in the United States, Canada, and Puerto Rico. It remains to be seen what this change will have, but the intent is to prevent a concentration of a few bloodlines to the detriment of the breed. The official rules read as follows:

(1) *For stallions born in 2019 and earlier, there will be no limit to the number of mares reported bred in the United States, Canada, and Puerto Rico. The Jockey Club will issue stallion certificates for all mares bred by such stallions within the United States, Canada, and Puerto Rico during a calendar year.*

(2) *For stallions born in 2020 and later, the maximum number of mares covered within the United States, Canada, and Puerto Rico in a calendar year will be 140. It would be a violation of Rule 14C for such a stallion to cover more than 140 mares within the United States, Canada, and Puerto Rico during a calendar year. The aforementioned limit will apply to all mares bred during a calendar year regardless of when The Jockey Club receives a Report of Mares bred (or any amendments or supplements thereto).*

Technology has facilitated the breeding process by enabling veterinarians to ascertain the mare's ovulation within a small window of time, thus requiring fewer covers to achieve more pregnancies. Stallion contracts generally specify that the stud fee is due by September or October first, but there are a multitude of propositions offered these days. Some commercial operations will even guarantee a specific return on your money should you sell the resulting foal with them, which is an idea you might consider if you wish to take on breeding as a venture.

No matter what their actual foaling date, Thoroughbreds are assigned a universal birthday of January 1 for purposes of The Jockey Club registration. Given the 11-month gestation period for a foal, the breeding season each year will begin around February 10. This is to avoid having a foal delivered in December and be at a disadvantage against horses born earlier in the year.

Such manipulation of Thoroughbred age and the resulting February start of breeding season is out of sync with the natural rhythms of mares, whose estrus, or "heat"cycle, occurs with the most regularity from April to August in the Northern Hemisphere. Modern technological advances have seen to it that fertility rates have improved, and the advantage of being able to breed a mare precisely upon a natural ovulation cycle has made achieving a pregnancy much easier.

Still, many breeders incorrectly presume that the earlier their foal is born in the calendar year the more advantage they will have when they go to the sales or to race with what they believe is a more mature individual. But statistics fail to indicate that February foals have any particular advantage over those born in April or May.

As recently as 2019, the first three horses to cross the finish line in the Kentucky Derby were all late May foals, which meant that none of them were even a full three years of age when they competed in America's premier race for three-year-olds. As mentioned in Chapter 4, one of the breedings I arranged for Due Process resulted in a Northern Dancer filly born on July 4, and she managed to win one of the Maryland Million stakes races. Some breeders will tell you that it's usually better to have a late foal than no foal at all, since a good horse will overcome many obstacles, including being the youngest kid in the class. At most stallion stations, the breeding shed will remain open until the fourth of July, and if your mare is cycling, you will have a good possibility of getting her in foal in June to allow for a May delivery the following year.

It is unusual that a mare will be able to produce a live foal every year. Most horsemen consider a mare that can foal three out of every four years during her breeding career to be outstanding. However, that does not stop many breeders from doing their utmost to get a foal from a mare every year.

Many horsemen feel that your best chance for finding a stakes horse is with a mare's first foal, or one born the year after she has taken a year off. Some discerning buyers use that rule of thumb as a criterion when digging through the thousands of yearlings offered every season.

It also has been proven that a mare can be tricked into ovulating earlier than the natural season if she is kept under lights. Trainers at the track, as well as mare and stallion managers, all keep the lights on in their stalls up to twenty-four hours a day in the effort to encourage this adaptation. This has proven effective in encouraging the mares to cycle regularly, but keep in mind that Mother Nature has a way of overruling our best efforts. The most effective plan is always to rely on the natural heat period to breed your mare.

Regular monitoring either by ultrasound or manual palpation is necessary to insure the mare's health. Closed circuit cameras allow the manager in charge to monitor the mares. Some will use an alarm apparatus attached to the mare to predict the impending arrival of the foal. Be forewarned that although your mare may have been pronounced "in foal," and the early ultrasound examination has ruled out the undesirable possibility of twins, there are numerous other caveats. Approximately five percent of mares that conceive will lose the fetus 30-90 days into their pregnancy. This is referred to as "slipping," resorption, or abortion.

Many mares which have come from the track and most which have been bred will have had their vulva sewn shut to prevent "wind sucking," whereby they draw air and detritus into their vagina and risk either infection or the chance of abortion. This procedure, called a Caslick's surgery, is often done when a mare has a tipped vulva which can allow feces to drop into or leak into their vagina and possibly render the mare infertile.

When the mare begins to show signs of nearing delivery, such as a waxing of her nipples or beginning to drip milk, the foaling person (or crew, depending on the size of the operation) will move her to a stall specifically designated for the birth. Many farms use oversized stalls with padded floors and walls and have them outfitted with closed circuit cameras to monitor the mare around the clock. Their veterinarian will be on call, but the time he takes to get to the farm can be critical in the case of a problem delivery, like an abnormal or breech presentation. Often a mare can be exhausted by the process of labor, and the foaling crew will assist in the birth by actually pulling out the foal. Caesarean deliveries to save a foal are extremely rare and done only in the face of complications that could result in loss of both mare and foal.

Upon delivery, the foal is checked to see if they have absorbed antibodies from their mother's milk, called colostrum, and given an enema to promote gastro-health. Amazingly, most foals will take to their feet less than an hour after their birth and begin nursing. It's quite a sight. The first three days of a foal's life are considered the most critical in terms of survival, as any prenatal and perinatal infections will evidence themselves at this time. Also, any physical defects that may need treatment will be readily apparent.

Then the process begins again. Sending a mare to be bred on the nine-day heat – known as the foal heat – immediately after she has delivered a foal is a controversial topic. If the foal heat breeding is successful, it shortens the time until the next foaling, thus keeping the mare "on schedule." If unsuccessful, the time between deliveries can be as much as 372 days, which means the mare's foaling date becomes later each year. Since things have a way of not going as planned in the breeding world, and even the best mare will eventually need a year off, this is not necessarily a bad thing at all.

Within a few days of foaling, most mares can be resutured and ready for teasing to ascertain their suitability for breeding. Since mares will only be receptive to being bred when they are in heat, a teaser horse is used to determine their readiness. And because the stallion ranks highest in the pecking order of the breeding world and his health cannot be risked, a lesser male must stand in to tease the mares. Referred to as the worst job in the business, the teaser may enjoy the foreplay, nuzzling, and arousal, but then he is promptly dismissed and never allowed to complete the sexual act.

After the mare comes in heat, the veterinarian will manually palpate her by donning a plastic sleeve to insert his arm and feel her ovaries. They may also use a speculum or an ultrasound for the examination. Should the vet decide she is ready, the farm manager or broodmare manager will call the stallion station and make an appointment for the breeding. Ideally, your mare will get the exact time and date she needs, depending on the time of the season and how many mares the stallion is covering. Hopefully she will be bred within twenty-four hours before ovulation, which is the ideal time, as mares bred after ovulation have a lower rate of conception.

Since mares tend to repeat their breeding patterns, the stallion manager will keep precise records of their behavior. And because mares may move from one farm to another over a period of years, these charts can prove invaluable.

Unlike other racing breeds, artificial insemination is not permitted in the Thoroughbreds. This adherence to the natural act of procreation requires the mare and stallion go through a pre-coital regimen that includes washing, the wrapping of the mare's tail wrapped with gauze, and possibly the use of hobbles attached to her legs or padded boots on her hind legs to prevent her from kicking the stallion out of fear or anticipation. In the case of a mare which has recently foaled, her foal will remain behind at the farm so as not to be a distraction.

The mating process is usually videotaped and requires several attendants, one stallion handler with one or two assistants, another for the mare, plus a veterinarian. The team makes sure the stallion properly mounts the mare and signals ejaculation by "flagging" his tail. In the case of a shorter stallion and a tall mare, the stallion will have a small hill similar to a pitcher's mound to stand on in order to help him mount. The stallion attendant or vet will collect some of the excess ejaculate post-breeding, and the rules do allow for its insertion, called "reinforcing," via a syringe to increase the chances of conception. Most farms also allow a repeat cover, called "doubling" within 48 hours of the first breeding if the stallion is available.

The general procedure is for the vet to perform an examination at 14 days by inserting a probe into the mare rectally and taking an image of her uterine horns which will show the fetus. Since the normal cycle of a mare is comes each 18 to 21 days, if the mare has not come back in heat at 18 days after the breeding you have a pregnant mare. Subsequent examinations at 26-30 days will show the beating heart of the fetus.

After a veterinarian has checked the pregnant mares, they are divided into groups according to their projected foaling dates. Depending on the size of the farm, in early December a foaling crew will begin to monitor the mares in a barn which includes an oversized foaling stall specifically for the birthing. The process of separating pregnant mares their suckling foals is called "weaning," and therefore the point at which the foals become known as weanlings.

Weaning the foal from its mother is a significant event in the life of both. When the foal is five or six months old it is time to separate them, and as you can imagine, this is a stressful process that needs careful consideration. A skilled broodmare manager in charge of many mares will begin to take a few of them from the field at feeding time while their foals are distracted with their grain or sweet feed. Usually, the foals don't notice the mother's absence right away. The burden of the stress falls on the mare when she realizes her baby is no longer with her, and the two are separated by enough distance that neither can hear the other's cries. For many years *The Blood-Horse* magazine carried the astrological signs of the zodiac, allegedly a guide to weaning time. Old time breeders swore by the method, but I don't know anyone who does it anymore, although I imagine someone will soon come up with an "app" so you can wean by your iPhone.

The broodmare manager will evaluate the weaned foals for physical defects and divide them further if they need appropriate treatment according to dietary restrictions. Many use this time to decide if the foals should be culled if they do not fit with the owner's long-term program. You might be better off eliminating the ones with conformation defects early by putting them in the mixed November or January sales rather than continue the expenses of board and upkeep. Weanlings are also separated by sex, either at weaning time or at the first of the following year, depending on the numbers at the farm. They gain independence as they mature, and by spring of their yearling year, you will know if you have a suitable horse for the sales ring or the racetrack.

There is a tendency among breeders to treat your horse like one of the family. Do not overbreed your mare simply because you can afford to. Unless she has won a Grade I stakes or a string of Grade IIs and IIIs, you should not be breeding to leading stallions with a price tag over $100,000 simply because you have deep pockets. Keep this guideline in mind: A foal should bring three times the stud fee required to produce it. If you breed your well-bred, non-stakes winning mare to a stallion whose stud fee exceeds her value, you will likely lose money if you decide to sell that foal, unless it is conformationally outstanding.

Another John Madden caveat worth repeating concerns homebreds, which he considered better than commercially bred horses because they grow up naturally, without the pressures of the market hanging over their heads. Madden would likely be rolling over in his grave if he knew the array of cosmetic surgeries and prophylactic treatments used to prepare modern "hot-house"yearlings and two-year-olds for the market.

"Wide range of pasture and long hours in the open are the best treatment for yearlings," Madden said. "They may not be so attractive to the eye on sales day but will not be so likely to bring disappointment to their owners afterward."

As one can see from the stallion rosters filled with studs offered at nominal fees or on fee-less deals every season, nearly all stud farms have too many stallions. As in buying fine wine, price can be a prime indicator of quality, but it ain't necessarily so. A time-tested fact of life in the horse breeding world dictates that only one of every 10 stallions in every price category will breed to expectations during their first five years. If they don't, their stud fee will drop dramatically until it reaches the fair market value. An outstanding runner like Alysheba went to stud at $50,000, and within a few years he could be had for $10,000 when he failed to produce any offspring of stakes quality. Others, like Storm Cat, Danzig, and Deputy Minister, started at $20,000 or $25,000 and were blessed with stakes quality offspring in their first two or three crops, escalating their stud fees to well over the $100,000 mark. Current top stallions Tapit and Into Mischief continue to illustrate this pattern, having started their breeding careers at $15,000 and $12,500, respectively.

If you are breeding to sell, you'll find that the least desirable season to breed to any stallion is his second year at stud, primarily because the yearling you bring to the market will rely on the race performance of the stallion's first crop. If they are duds, you'll be selling against unfavorable statistics. For just this reason, expect a discount on many stallions in their second season, should you be willing to take that risk.

Finally, do not assume that because you are an astute handicapper and pick plenty of winners that you can do the same in the breeding game. Volumes have been written explaining the complexity of the art, or science, of Thoroughbred breeding. But if the task could be reduced to a simple equation or be spit out by a computer program, anyone could breed a champion. Keep in mind that pedigrees appear on paper, but superior racehorses only appear on the track, and the greatest asset you have is your team of advisors.

Since, as Madden noted, the stud is responsible for 75 percent of the foal's chance to be a racehorse, it's easy to recognize that most of the value in Thoroughbred breeding is on the stallion side. The only way to really beat the game is to produce a stallion and have him go on to achieve greatness in the breeding shed.

Considering that all the top stallions need to have on average a fertility rate of over 80 percent in order to produce enough offspring to make the annual list, simple math illustrates the extraordinary rewards to those who own them.

A top-tier stallion standing for $100,000, multiplied by 100 successfully foaling mares, will produce a gross return of $10 million. Should they make it to the top five stallions, their stud fee can reach a quarter of a million dollars or more, generating upwards of $25 million from covering those 100 mares. Even the stallions further down the list, standing for $10,000 to $25,000, can produce many millions should the farm be able to promote them successfully.

Coolmore Stud in Ireland has had the most successful run with champion stallions. Their 14-time leading sire Sadler's

Wells was followed by his son, Galileo, whose four Epsom Derby winners and 84 Grade I winners made him the world's best stud. Both stallions garnered stud fees of over 300,000EU and bred books of mares numbering between 100 and 150, easily returning 25-30 million Euros annually to the coffers of Coolmore Ireland. They also perfected the practice of dual hemisphere breeding, and their Kentucky and Australia operations have enabled them to double and triple those figures while they reinvested in American Triple Crown winners American Pharoah and Justify, each starting their careers with stud fees in excess of $100,000 and capable of reaching the top of the stallion lists in seasons to come.

Taking into consideration the most simplistic approach, one can see the obvious advantages in breeding to proven stallions. The most successful breeders also factor in the stallion's ability to produce quality daughters who in turn produce winning racehorses, thereby enhancing the reputation of a stallion as a "broodmare sire." As illustrated by the amount of winning purses garnered by chief earners, the contribution of a quality sire with a quality mare can result in what we're all looking for: a superior runner.

There's nothing brighter than the smiles of big race winners.

CHAPTER 8

GAME PLANS

"Life is too short to make bad decisions ... and so is the racing season."

~ *J. Perrotta*

It is not uncommon to hear a newcomer to the racing game expound on a successful career in their chosen profession and firmly state their intention to operate their Thoroughbred stable just like they did their previous endeavor.

"Got to run it like a business," they'll say. "It's just another business, so I'll run it like one."

They have the right idea. Unfortunately, it is not uncommon that they fail to follow through. Details are overlooked or ignored, and soon they find out how many small leaks it takes to sink a mighty ship – especially a ship sailing on a sea of invested capital that can be twice as much as the purse money they can possibly win.

In 2000, it was estimated that owners only recouped 42 percent of the expense of horse ownership, a harsh reality that does not even include purchase prices. The percentage has not changed significantly over the first decades of the 21st century. Once again, consider that you are going against the odds at the outset, and that all the variables that make horseracing so fascinating must be overcome to succeed.

Industry experts agree that the total annual investment for the purchase of racehorses has exceeded the $2 billion mark. The annual purse pool for U.S. racing is a little more than half that $2 billion figure, meaning the majority of owners of horses competing in any calendar year probably will lose money – especially if they fail to follow the rules set forth in their *Thoroughbred Investor's Bible.*

As noted in earlier chapters, it is a cold fact of the racing game that if you are winning races 15 to 18 percent of the time, you are miles more successful than most of your competition. This can be a difficult pill to swallow for those inclined to look at the numbers as losing at a rate of more than 80 percent. In many businesses, this would be a recipe for disaster. Imagine a restaurant that only showed a marginal profit 75 days a year and lost money the rest of the time? Most likely they are soon out of business.

To avoid the racing disappointments that can lie in wait, you should be prepared to devise a business plan at the outset of your investment that states in black and white both short and long-term objectives. Do you want to win the Kentucky Derby? A Breeders' Cup? Get in the winner's circle with your friends at your local track? Breed a horse and watch it grow? Focus on your goals and consult your master plan often to make certain it is being followed.

The essential components of a business plan begin with an estimated budget and a timetable to achieve specific parameters of success. Make sure these elements are realistic, along with your commitment to personal participation in the project.

To reiterate important lessons from Chapter 3, the advisor that you select must understand your plan and be able to counsel you on your methodology for assembling the stable. This includes the acquisition of your horses – whether through claiming, private purchase, public auctions, or breeding – and establishing an efficient and consistent procedure for communi-

Million-dollar yearlings attract all the attention.

cation. Most of all, your advisor must be aware of the specifics of your budget. It does no good to set out to the Keeneland yearling sale to bid on horses that do not suit either your plan or your pocketbook.

In addition to your bloodstock advisor and your trainer, a highly valuable addition to your team should be a racing-savvy legal counsel. (Your accountant/tax advisor/CPA is another key player and will be discussed extensively in Chapter 10.) You likely already have an attorney capable of dispensing advice on your business, real estate, or personal affairs, but once again we must note that the horse racing game has its own language and set of rules. Keep your personal attorney, but take your equine advice from a specialist, and endeavor to learn the language of racing if you expect to receive any measure of respect from your new peers.

Nothing is more telling of a newcomer than incorrect use of specific terminology. As an example, one you hear often refers to a horse as being "out of" a stallion. Offspring are "by" the sire and "out of" the dam, which, when you think of it in literal terms, makes perfect sense.

Because highly specific terminology may appear in syndicate agreements when buying into racing or stallion groups, it is better to take counsel from someone who already understands the language. Keep in mind that racing attorneys have seen many of these agreements. If you are considering starting your own partnership or syndicate, they probably have one that can be customized to your needs. If nothing else, this will cost a lot less than starting from scratch.

There are two books I would recommend as a worthy investment in your early racing education: *The Complete Equine Legal and Business Handbook,* by Milton Toby, and *Equine Legal Handbook,* by Gary Katz.

Both include sample agreements for private sale and purchase of horses and various versions of standard partnership and syndicate agreements, as well as stock agreements for boarding, breeding, and leasing of racehorses and breeding stock. All of these agreements can be necessary in the syndication of stallions and racing stock, private acquisition, and representation at public auction and pinhooking operations.

Another excellent source of information for your bookshelf is *Equine Law,* by Frank T. Becker, which is described as a "comprehensive treatise on equine law as it relates to racehorses," covering such areas as purchase and sale, co-ownership, syndication, and management as well as legal issues relating to injuries caused by horses and the legal consequences of mistreatment of horses.

On one point all these sources will agree: *whatever you do, put it in writing.*

Like any other business environment, the equine world will occasionally present legal challenges. Equity ownership disputes, purse disputes, medication positives, disputes over questionable business practices, and the contesting of debatable stewards' rulings all would be situations that require the services of an attorney.

The outcome of a race is one example in which you might find yourself needing counsel. Take, for example, the result of the 2019 Kentucky Derby, in which Maximum Security was disqualified from first and runner-up Country House elevated to victory. Gary West, the owner of Maximum Security, was not able to challenge the stewards' decision under Kentucky rules, so he took the rules themselves to court in an attempt to overturn the disqualification of his horse. Two rulings against him and 15 months later, West finally gave up his pursuit of a reversal.

Where do you find an attorney with specialized horse racing knowledge? In fact, there are many equine law specialists working in different parts of the country – especially Kentucky – and if you want to find one in your area, a sales company can put you in touch, or you can interview some of those listed in *The Source*, published by *Blood-Horse*. As examples, I can mention two individuals I have known and consider extremely able practitioners.

Andrew "Drew" Mollica spent a decade working as a jockey agent on the East Coast circuit representing such Hall of Fame riders as Jose Santos and Chris Antley. Rather than continuing to haunt the backstretch hustling for mounts, Mollica made a career shift to serve members of the racing community as an attorney. Mollica's practice represents owners and trainers in a variety of cases, as well as jockeys wishing to contest their riding suspensions.

Darrell Vienna was once a bull rider, working the rodeo circuit and living the cowboy life before settling in as one of

California's finest trainers. Based in Southern California, Vienna sent out horses to earn more than $50 million. Included among them were Gilded Time, winner of the Breeders' Cup Juvenile and champion two-year-old male of 1992. Like Mollica, Vienna earned his law degree late in life, and eventually retired completely from training to represent racetrack clients full-time.

I refer to these individuals I have known as illustrations of the type of person you want on your team, well versed in the game with a depth of experience. Others of good repute and excellent experience that you may wish to consider are Bing Bush of Del Mar, Calif., and Mike Meuser of the Miller, Griffin and Marks practice in Lexington, Ky. Clark Brewster of Tulsa, Okla., is another attorney who knows his way around equine issues. He also operates his own ranch and training center while racing horses nationwide.

Even when all of your players are in place – advisor, trainer, attorney, accountant, etc. – your horse racing business plan will face variables unique to the industry. That is because you are dealing with animals, and animals must be recognized as having their own agenda.

Realistically, for everything that can go right, a dozen things can go wrong. Mares could fail to conceive, or when they do, they might abort, or produce a foal with crooked legs. Stallions slip and fall or get kicked by a mare and are rendered unable to perform their stud duties. Weanlings and yearlings at play can beat each other up or spook from a wild animal in the night and run through a fence, suffering a range of injuries. While training in the morning, racehorses have been known to dump their riders and gallop loose through the stable area endangering their lives and the lives of others, perhaps running into a pickup truck, resulting in wounds requiring multiple stitches and compromising their chance of making it to the races.

Horses can also train like champions until that day they begin to make a certain noise while breathing hard, perhaps necessitating a throat operation which may or may not solve the problem. They can win a race and leave the winner's circle limping, only to have X-rays reveal a career ending fracture.

How do I know about all these horrible tales? Am I trying to scare you away? Not at all, but I have experienced each and every one of those setbacks, large and small, at one time or another. And yet I haven't quit.

Those who love the game are inspired to take the chances, factor in the risks, and plan for success, for there is only one proven course of action that can help you rise above the potential setbacks: Control the elements of the business plan that you can control – such as costs, bookkeeping, accounting, agreements, personnel, and communication – then understand and accept the fact that the chance your horses will cooperate might be slim. In addition, it never hurts to hope the "racing gods" smile upon you with some luck, for there is nothing like the exhilaration experienced when the plan works, either in breeding and selling a valuable yearling or training a fast racehorse to win at your favorite track.

As a friend used to say, it's a great game if you can outlast the pain.

So, back to practicalities. Start by fine-tuning your business plan along specific, proven guidelines that answer some fundamental questions.

Should you buy colts or fillies?

My personal preference, especially for new investors in Thoroughbreds, is to start by purchasing fillies with some acceptable level of pedigree, at least the best your budget will allow. Keep in mind that the best chances for return on investment in horses is in the breeding end of the game. Male horses, although they are able to breed multiple times and possess the most potential, also carry the most risk.

All acquisitions, colts or fillies, should adhere to a few guidelines. For instance, when buying a weanling, never pay more than three times the stud fee. This is the ratio most commercial sellers consider when budgeting their income. Yearling prices should be slightly higher and two-year-olds in training higher still, since the seller's capital investment has grown accordingly.

Male horses bring the most money at auctions, since a successful stallion career can go on for decades and return huge returns. But a horse has to earn the right to become a stallion, and before that happens, he may go physically wrong and become worthless as an investment, while a female with a decent pedigree always will have broodmare potential. In fact, many male horses require gelding (castration) to achieve their best chance as racehorses. And the value of a gelding at career's end? Zero, unless he is adaptable to a new career as a show horse, jumper, or riding horse.

Investment in fillies at the weanling or yearling stage is often the best strategy for new owners. You can buy a big pedigree at a discount if you can accept a slight conformational flaw or something that discourages your vet about their future as a racehorse. You would be taking a chance that the horse in question could overcome their perceived problems, but there have been many superior runners who have outgrown cosmetic flaws by training and racing to their intrinsic ability.

On the other hand, I have purchased yearling fillies by top sires and of considerable potential only to find out when they were put into training that they were either too slow, unable to be motivated, or had an injury that ended any chance of a racing career. Once I sent them to the breeding shed, however, several of these "failures" turned out to be the dams of stakes winners and produce six-figure offspring the sales.

Even though fillies and mares with solid pedigrees are potential broodmares, their output is limited to one foal a year, and not every year is guaranteed. Even a mare with an excellent produce record may fail to conceive one out of every four years. In short, stallions might be the machinery, but the mares are the factory, and your factory must produce enough profit in the active years to offset the lack of income in the non-productive ones.

What about insurance?

How much and what kind is appropriate for a horse operation depends primarily on your financial situation, and there is always the conundrum of how much insurance is too much, or not enough.

Equine insurance is divided into three broad categories: 1) racehorses, 2) broodmares, foals, and yearlings, and 3) stallions. Rates are based on the age of the horse and bundling with a deductible. As with any insurance policy, your tolerance for risk will allow you a lower premium. The only problem with including lesser valued horses on a deductible policy is that if they die, you may satisfy the deductible amount but still not receive any settlement and still be out the premium. Some investors may wish to self-insure rather than pay premiums, depending on their budget and their tolerance for risk.

Racehorses are generally insured at approximately five per-cent of their value – value being a relative concept that may fluctuate based on the horse's performance or the performance of their close kin. Insurers came up with the concept of "agreed value," whereby the owner and insurer agree in advance on the individual animal's value and adjust on a race-to-race basis. There are a number of equine appraisers who can provide a detailed analysis and approximate value of your stock. Once again, you can find them in the *Blood-Horse's Source*.

Racehorses are only insured for full mortality, with loss of use not considered unless you negotiate a special deal at a higher rate. Thus, a horse may become useless for racing or breeding by a bowed tendon or a non-fatal fracture, but their insurance coverage can only be collected should they die. Otherwise, the owner is still on the hook for board and ongoing veterinary costs. Obviously, the risk to racehorses in training is greater than it is to broodmares spending their time in open paddocks with little physical jeopardy. The rates reflect this difference, as well as on the age of the mare.

You can insure just about any horse or situation, from simple mortality to loss of use to stallion infertility. Keep in mind, though, that insurance is really a bet against yourself. Depending on the value of any particular horse in the stable, the decision needs to be made as to whether its loss would affect the overall business plan. Some stables insure every single horse, all the way to ordinary claimers, while other stables don't insure a horse valued at less than seven figures.

At every horse sale there can be found reliable, experienced equine insurance agents available to work with you and craft a policy to suit your plan. As all agents ultimately go through the same insurance firms – Lloyds of London and Generali – your relationship with your agent is what you are paying for. The best agent will keep you apprised of the value of your stable if it changes, along with premium due dates and options for the best coverage. Again, find them in the *Source* and interview a few.

Broodmares and their foals are generally insured at approximately three percent of their value, depending on age. The mare rate increases based on actuarial tables and accelerates dramatically after they pass age 12. Unlike racehorses, mares may be insured for major medical coverage, including vet charges and surgery as a result of accident, injury or illness, even those incurred during delivery. Since their risk of injury or death is considerably low in the farm environment, many breeders self-insure, unless the mare has significant value.

Prospective foal insurance may be purchased if the mare is bred to a stallion with no guarantees, which describes the type of stud fee arrangements that became all the rage beginning in the late 1980s. You paid your money, sent your mare, and took your chances. In recent years most stallion stations have reverted to the industry standard of "live foal guaranteed to stand and nurse." The resulting foals may be insured at a sliding rate that declines as the foal ages.

Yearlings are either insured at an agreed value based on their stallion's stud fee and a percentage of the mare's value or, in the case of those yearlings purchased at auction, the price at the fall of the auctioneer's hammer. If you intend to buy at auction, discuss your plans with your insurance agent before the sale, and he will agree to cover you from the moment the sale is consummated.

Stallions, unlike other stock, can be covered for loss of use because their value can be quantified by multiplying their book of mares by their stud fee. Usually, such insurance is included in the cost of maintenance, which the syndicate or the farm bills the individual shareholders. In the case of first season stallions, it will cover infertility, as it did in the case of two-time Horse of the Year Cigar, who was sold for $25 million for a 75 percent share to Coolmore's American operation. Infertility in stallions is an uncommon occurrence, but the insurance is the only thing that will save you when it does happen. Another example is the case of Kentucky Derby winner and champion War Emblem, whose lack of success in the breeding shed was attributed to an absence of libido.

How do I decide when to sell?

It is important to continually assess the horses in your stable. You must commit to making hard decisions and apply your business principles, and you must do it on a disciplined annual basis to eliminate the horses that no longer fit the plan. Although there is always an emotional component to participation in horse racing, it is important, as a business practice, to never "fall in love" with any horse.

It is hard to let go and sell a horse who has provided entertainment and maybe even profit, but you must do so when it is time. This is referred to as culling. Quality is ultimately the only thing that counts, so keep in mind that the horse who just won the Kentucky Derby eats the same amount as the one who finished last in a maiden claimer. You cannot stay in business very long if you don't sell your goods, whether they are horses, automobiles, or antiques.

Public auction rules allow the vendor to place a reserve price on their horses for sale. When the bidding exceeds that reserve number, the horse will be sold to the highest bidder. Unless you are comfortable racing that horse and paying the maintenance, continuing to increase your capital investment, my personal preference is to set the reserve at an amount in the area of 60 percent of the price you feel is reasonable. You are still allowed to bid on your own behalf after the bidding exceeds that amount and you feel the need to protect yourself, keeping in mind that if you are the last bidder, you'll still own the horse.

Like any other sale subject to negotiating, you never want to fail to consummate a deal when you get close to your desired number. Buying your horse back at sales and taking them to another sale is a great deal for the auction company and the consignor, who would still charge their commission based on the buy-back price, but every time you do so you are only cutting your own throat with unrealistic expectations.

When considering whether to sell, we've all heard the trope that you never go broke taking a profit. The buyer may reap further rewards in a resale, but if you get a square price for the horse when you sold it, you are in keeping with another piece of wisdom from John Madden, who said, "It is better to sell and regret than to keep and regret." Write this rule on your wall, carve it in your desk, or have it tattooed on your forearm.

In buying, as in selling, there are steadfast rules that should be followed. Among them:

Do not buy a horse that is back at the knee.

This is a conformational defect that places undue strain on the soft tissue of the lower leg. Yes, there are examples of good horses that were exceptions. But as trainer John Tammaro, Jr., liked to say about horses with injured tendons, "Give them away to someone you don't like, and in the end, you'll be way ahead of the game."

Other undesirable traits that one should avoid are habits like cribbing (wind-sucking), weaving (horses that sway on their forelegs, shifting weight back and forth as they move their head from side-to-side), and stall-walking. These habits are not intrinsically harmful to the horse, but they might indicate mental weakness or lead to other ailments.

Do not buy a horse that you or your advisor have not touched.

Inspect all prospective purchases before you bid and use all the tools available. Those include access to the veterinary repository, sales history guidebooks, and physical vetting by your own representative. There is no excuse for buying a horse with a poor walk, poor conformation, or a bad temperament. Even in today's age of internet sales and video breeze-up shows, I would still caution against buying a horse you have not seen up close and personal. You could be playing into the adage of buying a pig in a poke, when a "poke" was a sack, and the pig of uncertain quality was wriggling unseen inside.

Never pay too much for a pinhook.

These are horses bought at one sale specifically for the purpose of being sold at another. With some exceptions, the first one investing in a horse bought for resale usually makes the most profit, paid for by those looking to purchase a closer to race-ready product. It bears repeating that, as a rule, yearlings bring more than weanlings, two-year-olds in training bring more than yearlings, and winning racehorses bring the most. Horses closest to a race bring the most money, since all the hard work is behind them and most of the risk of injury during early training has been taken out of the equation.

Finally, as you are building your business plan, always bear in mind that horses are all maintenance, all the time. They must eat and be cared for every day, whether or not they are able to run when you want them to in order to generate some kind of return on your investment. They have a propensity to become injured, infirm, or ill, and they will test your patience in ways you have never experienced before. If you can't wait, they will make you wait. It is your responsibility to have both the plan and the attitude to make that wait worthwhile.

Terry Finley hoists a Derby trophy for his West Point partners.

CHAPTER 9

A GAME TO BE SHARED

*"It's better to own part of a good horse than to own all
of a bad one."*

~ Arnold Kirkpatrick

For as long as people have been following their dreams of
building and creating, innovating and inventing, there has been
a need to raise capital to achieve those dreams. The horse game
is no different. The laws of supply and demand dictate that the
strong survive and the big fish continue to thrive at the expense
of everyone else.

So how not to be swallowed by big fish like Coolmore,
Juddmonte, the Phipps family, etc.? Partnerships and
syndicates offer an answer in today's racing market, even
though they have existed in North America for decades. The
concept of disparate investors combining their resources to
acquire shares in a Thoroughbred of great value came to the
fore in 1956 when Kentucky breeder Leslie Combs II raised
$1,251,200 to purchase 1955 Horse of the Year Nashua from the
estate of William Woodward, Jr. Combs then leased the horse
from the syndicate and raced him in his colors for the
remainder of the 1956 season, after which Nashua was retired
to stud at Combs' Spendthrift Farm in Lexington.

The advantage to such a group participation in the
ownership of the champion was threefold: First, it mitigated

the expense of standing a stallion, which included not only board and care of the horse but also marketing, promotion, and insurance. Second, the stallion's potential book of mares was guaranteed to be filled with quality mares provided by the syndicate members, who were each entitled to breed at least one mare each season, it being in their best interest to send as fine a candidate as possible. Third, syndicate members like Christopher J. Devine, a leading trader in U.S. government bonds, created a synergy of excitement around the stallion through their spheres of influence. The Nashua syndication also established a standard for the farm that was standing the stallion to receive two to four annual breedings.

The original syndicates constructed in the 1950s and '60s included 25 to 35 members. At the time, those were the numbers considered ideal in terms of how many mares the stallion should serve in a single breeding season. If the stallion was required to cover a mare two or three times, he might have to be successful with a high percentage of more than 100 covers. Subsequently, the science and technology associated with breeding has become more refined, and it is now possible to determine the time of ovulation more precisely. This allows the stallion to achieve just as many pregnancies but with fewer covers. The logical extension of such mare management finds modern stallions covering more than 100 mares, with upwards of a 90 percent fertility rate based on 120-130 covers, whereas 20 or 30 years ago the same results would have required in excess of 200 covers.

Combs' success with Nashua became the paradigm for stallion syndication. He struck again in 1970 with the $1.8 million stallion syndication of 1969 Kentucky Derby and Preakness winner Majestic Prince. In 1973, Seth Hancock of Claiborne Farm closed a record $6.08 syndication deal for 1972 Horse of the Year Secretariat, who made young Hancock look like a genius when the colt won the 1973 Triple Crown and another title as Horse of the Year. The ever-competitive Combs answered the Secretariat number with the $7.2 million syndication of 3-year-old champion Wajima at the end of 1975.

If there was ever a bargain stallion syndication, it would have to be the $2.4 million valuation of 1964 Derby and Preakness winner Northern Dancer by Windfields Farm, which came after he had his first two crops to the races. Those offspring included Nijinsky II, winner of the 1970 English Triple Crown, and Fanfreluche, the 1970 champion 3-year-old filly of North America.

Northern Dancer went on to sire 147 stakes winners from 645 named foals during his career at stud. Of his 488 starters, 368 were winners and 146 were stakes winners. He also accounted for 26 champions in both North America and Europe, where his sons and daughters became stars on the grass. Northern Dancer's strike rate of 26 percent stakes winners from starters remains the pinnacle of stallion performance. It is also the reason his stud fee grew from the original 10,000 Canadian dollars to a cool $1 million USD by 1985, much to the delight of those original syndicate members.

By nearly every measure, it is no contest: Northern Dancer is the champ.

The success of any stallion syndicate is dependent on the performance of the stallion's foals within the first two or three crops. Because of slow starts to those first offspring, many stallions have gone from flavor of the month at the yearling sales to passengers on planes bound for breeding farms in Turkey, Korea, or Uruguay, never to be heard from again.

It is also a fact of life in the breeding and racing world that many outstanding stallion prospects have turned out to be better on the track than in the sack, so to speak. Among the most notable are two-time Horse of the Year Cigar, champion sprinter Precisionist, Kentucky Derby winner War Emblem, multiple European champion El Gran Senor, and Champagne

Stakes winner A.P. Valentine. They were found so lacking in the breeding shed that their ownerships collected on infertility insurance policies.

In establishing the modern prototype for a stallion syndicate, Combs also flung open the doors for multi-owner partnerships in racehorses that would begin to flower in the 1970s.

Cothran "Cot" Campbell of Aiken, South Carolina is widely acknowledged as the pioneer of Thoroughbred racing syndicates in the creation of Dogwood Stable in 1971.

Campbell started with a smallish, crooked filly that he purchased for $5,000 at the 1971 Hialeah yearling sale and built his empire upon the three stakes wins with which she rewarded him and his investors. An iconoclast from the start, Campbell served his investors by creating a training center on a farm he developed from scratch on 422 acres in West Central Georgia, about sixty miles from Atlanta.

Campbell worked the Kentucky auction circuit like a vacuum cleaner salesman, and in a few years Dogwood was winning the kind of stakes races that attracted new investors with horses like Dominion, winner of the Bernard Baruch at Saratoga; Summer Squall, winner of the 1990 Preakness; and his daughter, Storm Song, the champion two-year-old filly of 1996. (Campbell was also a great raconteur and writer. I highly recommend his memoir, *Lightning in a Jar*, for an engaging story of the ups and downs of horse ownership from the syndicator's point of view.)

Others followed Campbell's lead. Heading the list are West Point Thoroughbreds, Eclipse Thoroughbred Partners, and Starlight Racing. Each of those partnerships earned more than $2 million dollars in 2018, for example, while several other entities topped $1 million. Today there are more than 75 active syndicates offering shared ownership of racehorses and breed-

Cot Campbell (rt.) shares a Belmont trophy with Mike Smith.

ing stock under various scenarios for all budgets (see Appendix 5).

Syndicates and partnerships provide a good way to get your feet wet by owning a leg rather than the whole horse. They are a way to spread your risk, and many savvy investors have used them as an educational experience before going out on their own. For others, the need to be in control of their investment without having to defer to partners outweighs the benefit of mitigating risk in partnership. Syndicates, though, provide a framework within which individuals can come and go without too much drama. Informal partnerships, on the other hand, can sometimes end in grief.

In 1991, Hall of Famer Nick Zito trained his first Kentucky Derby winner, a chestnut son of Alydar named Strike the Gold. The colt had been purchased the previous year at the Keeneland yearling sales for $500,000 by the partnership of B. Giles Brophy, William Condren, and Joseph Cornacchia, and he raced under the silks of their BCC Stable. The Derby smiles evaporated, though, as Strike the Gold failed to find the winner's circle in his next 12 starts. By the following May the BCC partners were in an acrimonious squabble, spending most of their time skirting slander as they fought over who should make the training decisions.

As usual in the horse business, this type of situation is settled in the sales ring, where the animal enters without a reserve price and all partners (or other interested parties) are free to bid on their own accounts. Strike the Gold brought $2.9 million when Condren and Cornacchia essentially bought out Brophy's share, and they all walked away not speaking well of each other.

If you feel that you will derive your highest satisfaction from self-directed participation, have sufficient assets, and don't wish to listen to someone else's opinion, there's a good possibility you should go it alone. If not, read on.

Terry Finley graduated from West Point in 1986 and briefly considered a long-term career in the military, but he decided instead to follow his dreams that led to the racetrack. Finley and his wife, Debbie, created West Point Thoroughbreds in 1991, following the model established by Cot Campbell. By the end of 2021, they were approaching 1,000 wins for their syndicate members, including Grade I victories by Twilight Eclipse and Awesome Gem, both earners of more than $2 million, and the mare Hard Not to Love, who was resold by West Point for $3.2 million.

The syndicate's early turning point came in 1996 when Big City Band became the first West Point stakes winner, but their mark in racing history became reality in 2007, when Flashy Bull took the Grade I Stephen Foster Stakes at Churchill Downs. West Point runners went on to capture five Grade I stakes over the next 60 days, and they sent five horses to the Breeders' Cup that year at Monmouth Park, finishing third with Awesome Gem to champion Curlin in the Classic. Then, in 2017, West Point Thoroughbreds reached the pinnacle of the sport as part of the ownership group who celebrated the victory of Always Dreaming in the Kentucky Derby.

When asked what spurred him to form the West Point syndicate, Finley replied, "I was the youngest of seven, and my father was a schoolteacher. He didn't have a lot of disposable income, but he took a small share in a horse, and I saw how much pleasure it gave him, just being in the game."

Finley created a network of industry specialists designed to service the syndicate shareholders and make West Point ownership both exciting and a pleasant social experience. Most West Point clients have been referrals from previous syndicate members, and Finley notes that many clients have gone on to start their own stables while continuing to participate in his.

"So far, we have a lot of happy customers," Finley said. "Winning helps."

Few come into the Thoroughbred racing game with a better background than Anna Seitz Ciannello. Her father, Fred Seitz, grew up on William Payne Thompson's Brookdale Farm in Lincroft, N.J., a significant Thoroughbred nursery built in the late 1800s by David Dunham Withers, one of the founders of Monmouth Park. Later leased to Harry Payne Whitney, Brookdale Breeding and Stock Farm would produce Regret, the first filly to win the Kentucky Derby, and Upset, the horse that spoiled the legendary Man o' War's unbeaten record.

Bequeathed to Monmouth County by Geraldine Thompson in 1967, the property became the home to Brookdale College. For several seasons in the mid-1970s I taught a summer school class at Brookdale entitled "Horse Racing 101" to groups of 30 to 40 students of the game. Amazingly, some of them still approach me at the races to reminisce, and we usually agree that although time has passed, much of the material we covered in those classes is still relevant.

After completing his military service in the U.S. Marines, Fred Seitz began a career in the Thoroughbred industry. He relocated to Versailles, Ky., to raise his family, and he honored his roots by calling his new stallion station Brookdale Farm, which became home to a score of top-class stallions, including Deputy Minister, Silver Deputy and Forrest Wildcat. Brookdale also made a name as the consigner of quality mares, foals, and yearlings, while the Seitz family distinguished itself by producing Keeneland and Fasig-Tipton sales toppers.

In 2012, Anna Seitz Ciannello decided to assemble a group to race a daughter of Saratoga stakes winner Ready's Image that she had purchased for $20,000. Named I'm Already Sexy, the filly would go on to win $760,000 in 10 visits to the winner's circle, including six stakes races, before she was retired and sold to Japanese buyers for $420,000 as a broodmare prospect.

"I had incredible interest from women, excited about the horses and the sport, but terrified of the process," Ciannello said. "We thought we'd do a few syndicates and have some fun, but it just took off."

Ciannello called her syndicate It's All About the Girls. In collaboration with noted Irish horsewoman Elaine "Legs" Lawlor, the IAATG syndicates enjoyed more success with Global Glamour, Yes to the Dress, Our Majesty, Chicas Amigas, and Sparkle'n'joy, all stakes winners which were sold on to breeders at the end of their racing careers.

Ciannello noted that she was pleasantly surprised at how much value her syndicate members derived from the social aspect of IAATG, above and beyond the joy of winning races and money.

"The partial ownership concept allows our participants to spread the risk, and our philosophy is to create friendships and have some fun," Ciannello said. "We have some members that love to dress up for races as they would for any social event, and the enthusiasm is contagious. Fortunately, some of the horses we've acquired have done really well by us."

An understatement if there ever was one.

West Point Stable and It's All About the Girls are only two examples of successful partnership/syndicates, there are many more that operate across North America. If you are considering the group ownership concept, you may be able to find one in your neighborhood, enabling you to visit the horses at a nearby track and get some hands-on experience along with the satisfaction of ownership.

Other notable ventures include Billy Koch and Gary Fenton's Little Red Feather Racing and Aaron Wellman's Eclipse Thoroughbreds, both headquartered in California, as well as Barry Irwin's internationally active Team Valor.

CJ Thoroughbreds was created by Corey Johnsen, former racing executive and owner of Kentucky Downs. Having worked with Johnsen in the early 2000s when he ran Lone Star Park and I was VP of Operations for Frank Stronach's Magna Entertainment, I would consider his integrity impeccable.

All the above groups have successful past performance records. Beyond them, I would encourage you to interview several from the list in Appendix 5 to find one that best suits your needs.

Sackatoga Stable, for instance, is the brainchild of Saratoga Springs, N.Y., businessman Jack Knowlton, who enlisted high school friends to form a claiming stable. When they lost their mare Bail Money in a claim, they decided to re-invest in a Distorted Humor gelding bred in New York with an oddly compelling name.

Trained by Barclay Tagg, Funny Cide would win the 2003 Kentucky Derby and Preakness for the fun-loving Sackatoga syndicate to reach the threshold of a Triple Crown title.

Unfortunately, he lost the Belmont Stakes, finishing third behind Empire Maker and Ten Most Wanted, but he later won the Jockey Club Gold Cup and retired with more than $3 million in earnings.

As the 2020s dawned, Funny Cide had become a fan favorite at the Kentucky Horse Park in Lexington. Back at the track, the Sackatoga brand led by Knowlton was enjoying success with a son of Constitution named Tiz the Law, who became the leading colt of his generation early in 2020 with victories in the Grade I Florida Derby and the classic Belmont Stakes that was run as the first leg of a Triple Crown season impacted by the coronavirus restrictions on sporting events. Knowlton was dealing with a different group of investors from Sackatoga's Funny Cide days, but when it came to the giddy feeling of winning major races, the song remained the same. And how sweet it was.

The government does not mind if you make a profit.

CHAPTER 10

TAXES – THEY'RE NO GAME

"In this world nothing can be said to be certain except death and taxes."

~ Benjamin Franklin

The information to be found in the following pages is so crucial to your success that I considered making it the first chapter. Savvy investors will understand the necessity of building their own game plan with Uncle Sam's Internal Revenue Code in mind, in order to minimize the potential impact of tax implications in the future as well as enhance their chances of financial success.

As you've recognized by now, I consider our dictum regarding the choice of your experts as the number one piece of advice. As was the case with selection of your racing/breeding advisor, your trainer, and your personal attorney, the same imperative applies in seeking out a CPA/tax advisor: Be sure you choose one well-versed in the Thoroughbred business.

Racing has its own wrinkles and twists, and although you may have had a relationship with your personal CPA for many years, it is unlikely they have the knowledge of one who specializes in horses. Fortunately, there are excellent firms on both coasts and in Kentucky as a resource, and you should be able to get a recommendation from your main advisor.

Based on my knowledge, as well as the opinions of other horsemen and owners, I believe few in the Thoroughbred game have more expertise in this arena than Leonard Green.

Green is a licensed New Jersey CPA with an MBA in taxation from NYU and a graduate of the Harvard Business School Owner/President Management Program. Green is also founder and chairman of New Jersey-based accounting and equine advisory firm The Green Group, which specializes in the racing world with more than 400 accounting clients in the Thoroughbred and Standardbred industries nationwide, providing services for partnerships, syndications, owners, trainers, and breeders.

Green has been involved in the Thoroughbred industry for more than 30 years as an owner, breeder, and consultant. He is the managing partner of DJ Stable, LLC, a successful racing operation which has won 2,400 races at 13 different racetracks. DJ Stable has bred and/or owned 80 stakes winners, including major stakes winners Jayhawk (who won the Breeders' Cup Juvenile Fillies and an Eclipse Award), Helium, (who ran in the 2020 Kentucky Derby), Songandaprayer, Do It With Style, Hoppertunity, Larkwhistle, November Snow, and Rhum. Green also has earned eight individual leading owner titles at four different racetracks, including Monmouth Park and The Meadowlands.

The following article, entitled "Hobby is a four-letter word," by Leonard Green and John Wollenberg, CPA Esq., his colleague at The Green Group, originally appeared in the Thoroughbred Daily News. Rather than lift a few quotes, I feel obligated to share it with you in its entirety, with the kind permission of the authors. Green and Wollenberg begin:

"The Thoroughbred industry is one of the ways to own a piece of sports. For those of us who enjoy competition but cannot afford the 'billion-dollar price tag' associated with the New York Yankees or Dallas Cowboys, 'the sport of kings' provides an opportunity to participate in sports at the highest levels.

"Due to a multiple number of variables, [horse racing] is considered to be a challenging and arduous business. Even the IRS considers this activity as an 'uphill battle' and, therefore, regulates it under a unique set of rules and codes.

"One example is the way the IRS extends the time horizon for profitability. The unique rule variations for our industry provide a more lenient landscape to prove that a) your racing and/or breeding operations are 'for profit', and b) that you are taking the required steps to provide yourself with the opportunity to accomplish a profit motive.

"There are two safe-harbor rules for determining if you have a for-profit business:

"Normal Rule. An activity is presumed to be a for-profit business if it produces positive taxable income (revenues in excess of deductions) for at least three out of every five years. Losses from the other years can be deducted because they are considered to be business losses as opposed to hobby losses.

"Special Rule. Specifically, for the horse industry includes that horse racing, breeding, training, or showing activities are presumed to be for-profit business if they produce positive taxable income in two out of every seven years.

"Taxpayers who can plan ahead to qualify for these safe-harbor rules earn the right to deduct their losses against their earned income from outside sources during unprofitable years.

Honest intent to make a profit rule. Even if you cannot qualify for one of the aforementioned safe-harbor rules, you may still be able to treat the activity as a for-profit business and rightfully deduct the losses. Basically, you must demonstrate an honest intent to make a profit. Factors that can prove (or disprove) such intent include:

"Spending enough time at your craft to prove that the activity is a business, and not a hobby. This includes the '500-

hour test,' which represents the minimum amount of time devoted to the business during the course of one calendar year."

Green and Wollenberg go on to list a variety of activities that would qualify toward satisfying the 500-hour test and have historically passed IRS scrutiny. They include:

--Conducting the activity in a businesslike manner by keeping detailed books and records.

--Discussions with trainers, jockeys, and other industry-related professionals, documented by phone calls, texts, emails, and meetings.

--Attendance at races, horse sales, and other industry-related activities.

--Complying with licensing and regulatory requirements.

--Reading trade publications.

--And any other work done in connection with the business, a catch-all category that basically equates to any other items not previously listed. The article continues:

"In order to best provide evidence of the above, we recommend that you annually provide your tax preparer with your horse-related calendars. This should include attended races, meetings, sales, etc.

"Be prepared to provide the IRS with proof of expertise and/or hiring a third-party service (i.e., attorney, accountant, bookkeeper, etc.) with years of experience working within the equine field. Evidence of such will add tremendous weight in circumstances such as an audit. Testament of success in other ventures will aid in indicating business acumen.

"The history and magnitude of income and losses from the activity can be important. Occasional large profits hold more weight than frequent small profits. Losses caused by unusual events or bad luck are more justifiable than ongoing losses that only a hobbyist would be willing to accept. Your financial status—the higher your net worth, the more likely you can afford to absorb ongoing losses (which may indicate a hobby).

"Elements of personal pleasure--attending stakes races is usually more fun than digging post holes for fences. However, the IRS is far more likely to claim the former is a hobby if losses start showing up on your tax returns.

"As an active member in the Thoroughbred industry, you are well aware of how difficult it is to be profitable. Thankfully the IRS also understands the difficulty of normal profitability standards.

"When you invest in the stock market, you rarely have to worry if General Mills had a bout with colic the night before a big event. However, when investing in delicate athletes, like Thoroughbreds, you are constantly worried about a plethora of factors. This can include their overall health, the track conditions, if they break from the gate alertly, if your yearling vetted out before a sale, if your mare carried her pregnancy full-term and countless other variables completely out of your control. Nonetheless, what is in your control, are following some of the above-mentioned guidelines to prove your intention for profit.

"It is in your best interest to attend sales, meet with your trainer regularly, talk sale strategy with your consignor and most importantly surround yourself with experts in the industry who have successful racing and breeding operations.

"The American Horse Council and the National Thorough-bred Racing Association both lobby relentlessly on behalf of the industry. Both recommend familiarity with the tax regulations as horseracing has its own peculiarities that must be recognized in reporting to the government. Their websites contain tax benefit and investment incentive information, updated monthly to keep pace with changes that may affect your decisions.

"The 2017 Tax Cuts and Jobs Act contains a number of items which benefit Thoroughbred horse and farm owners operating their horse and farm activities as businesses that use the cash method of accounting. Major elements of the changes include the reduction of tax rates for businesses and individuals, increasing the standard deduction and family tax credits, eliminating personal exemptions, and making it less beneficial to itemize deductions, limiting deductions for state and local income taxes and property taxes.

"Depreciation - general rule. Horses may be depreciated over three to seven years. Racehorses two years old and older and breeding stock over twelve are depreciated over three years. Based on actual date of birth, not the Jan. 1 Thorough-bred date. Effective of the 2017 Tax Cuts and Jobs Act, all others may be depreciated over seven years. If 40 percent of purchases are made in the last quarter, depreciation is reduced.

"It significantly expanded bonus depreciation by specify-ing that the percentage that may be currently deducted for tax purposes be increased to 100 percent of the purchase price for qualifying property placed in service through 2022. After 2022, the percentage drops by 20 percent each year until it becomes 20 percent in 2026. In addition, the definition of qualifying property was expanded to include assets that have been previously owned but not those being reacquired by the purchaser. Previously, assets used by a prior owner did not qualify.

"Equine assets that may qualify for this 100 percent write-off would include racing prospects, racehorses, broodmares and stallions as well as equipment, fencing, barns and improvements to the land and is not limited by taxable income. The deduction may be used as a net loss with no specific dollar amount limitation annually.

"The benefit of these changes outweighs the previously governing Section 179 depreciation, which was limited to net income and also to a fixed annual dollar amount. Most im-portantly, bonus depreciation also is not prorated based on the timing of the purchase and thus a qualifying purchase made and placed in service on Dec. 31 is eligible for the same amount of bonus depreciation as property purchased for the same price earlier in the year. In order to claim the bonus depreciation, the asset must be 'placed in service' during the tax year. For tax purposes, racing prospects may be placed in service either in the fall of the yearling year when training begins or when they begin racing.

"This change also benefits depreciation of breeding stock which may be placed in service even if the purchaser does not plan to breed the horse until the following year, or when bred, and also holds true for stallions or stallion shares.

"The method or timing of payment comes into play as well. Shares in a horse purchased as a stallion prospect while the horse is still racing would not be considered placed in service until the horse is retired from racing and available to be bred or begins breeding. On the other hand, a horse purchased and placed in training or racing but not yet paid for would be eligible for the bonus depreciation.

"Farms using bonus depreciation could realize a substantial portion of the purchase price being eligible for immediate deduction by specifying this allocation prior to purchase with the seller in the closing documents or using an appraisal that allocates a portion of the purchase price to these depreciable assets.

"If a yearling is purchased for $500,000, the whole $500,000 may be fully deducted in year 1 rather than the seven-year life, taken over an eight-year period as previous law allowed, resulting in a federal tax savings of $185,000 if the purchaser is in the highest federal individual tax bracket. By accelerating this deduction versus claiming it over time, the cash savings in this specific example is approximately $30,000 if a 5 percent rate of return is used.

"In the case that your horse business is otherwise profitable, you as the owner might wish to report a net profit for hobby loss rules that shifts the burden of proof to the IRS if profits are reported in two out of seven years or utilize the related depreciation expense better during the period of time that horses or the farm would produce income in future years. Passive investors in syndicates or partnerships may receive little tax benefit by accelerating this deduction and might create a state withholding tax issue in future years when purse winnings are generated or the horse is sold at a profit with no remaining tax basis.

"In some cases, one may wish to use 100 percent of the bonus depreciation on certain classes of assets while electing out of others deducting the depreciation on barns over the standard 20-year life while claiming the 100 percent write-off on horse purchases by opting out of the 20-year asset class only, keeping in mind that horses should be categorized appropriately with either a three-year or a seven-year life. Weanlings in general, either purchased for resale or to race, are not eligible as they have not been placed in service.

"Limitations. As with most other tax incentives, a few limitations that might currently reduce or eliminate this 100 percent deduction may apply. The tax law created a provision that limits net 2018 losses from all business ventures for individuals, trusts and estates to $250,000 ($500,000 for individuals filing jointly). This limit is indexed for inflation after 2018. Any net business loss that exceeds the limit is converted to a net operating loss.

"Bonus depreciation might significantly increase the net business loss generated and cause this business loss to be currently limited. For many industry participants who are affected, this creates a one-year deferral of this excess loss that then might be used to offset all sources of income in the subsequent year, subject to the normal net operating loss carryover rules. So, owners faced with excess business losses might still want to currently claim bonus depreciation.

"Another item of caution: Many states have decoupled from this favorable bonus depreciation so this may be a Federal tax benefit only, depending in which states a horse or farm owner operates.

"Each year a number of sales auctions occur. The 100 percent write-off option presents some planning opportunities for those looking to reduce taxable income. It is important to speak with your tax advisors regarding your specific situation prior to making any purchases, but the potential tax benefit of utilizing bonus depreciation could be substantial."

Finally, the authors address the holding period for calculating capital gains/losses:

"Unlike many other assets, the holding period to qualify for long term capital gains is two years. The maximum tax rate on long term capital gains is 20 percent vs. maximum income tax of 40 percent. Always check with your tax advisor as the tax law continuously changes."

Keep these lessons close at hand. It is the gospel at the heart of your *Thoroughbred Investors Bible.*

The modern-day Curragh still brims with great history.

CHAPTER 11

A GAME
WITHOUT BORDERS

"The Thoroughbred exists because its selection has depended, not on experts, technicians, or zoologists, but on a piece of wood: the winning post of the Epsom Derby."
                                                    ~ *Federico Tesio*

Taking their cue from Federico Tesio, the legendary Italian breeder of superhorse Ribot, American horsemen have long recognized the importance of European racing and the quality of European bloodstock, especially in England and France. Along those lines, any discussion of American breeding in the 20th century must begin with the Hancock family and descendants of Richard Hancock, a captain in the Confederate Army who served under Gen. Thomas "Stonewall" Jackson.

Having survived the Civil War, Hancock began to raise horses on his wife's family farm in Albemarle County, located in Northern Virginia. It was there he recognized the value of breeding domestic Thoroughbreds to superior European stock. In 1910, Hancock's son, Arthur B. Hancock, Sr., relocated the family operation to Kentucky. The son also married well, settling into the farm inherited by his wife, Nancy Tucker Clay, and naming their property Claiborne as an homage to his wife's family name.

Over the years, importation of the stallions Sir Gallahad III and Blenheim II from Europe went a long way toward changing the landscape of the American breeding industry. Among the offspring of Sir Gallahad III was Triple Crown winner Gallant Fox, while Blenheim II sired Triple Crown winner Whirlaway, among many other stakes runners. Arthur Hancock's success led the *British Bloodstock Review* to call him, "the most influential breeder in the history of the American turf," and the record supported the title. Hancock was the breeder of 138 stakes winners, including 10 champions. He was leading breeder by earnings five times, and co-breeder of 1947 Kentucky Derby winner Jet Pilot.

In the 1950s, Arthur "Bull" Hancock, Jr., succeeded his father as master of Claiborne. Bull Hancock stood Princequillo, who would lead the North American sire list in 1957 and 1958 and top the broodmare sire list an astonishing eight times between 1966 and 1976. Included among his successful daughters was Somethingroyal, who became the dam of Triple Crown winner and two-time Horse of the Year Secretariat. Hancock's other brilliant stallions included Double Jay, Round Table, Nasrullah, and Bold Ruler, the sire of Secretariat.

Hancock's success attracted many of the sport's wealthiest patrons. His relationships with the Phipps family of financiers, metals magnate Charles Engelhard, and Standard Oil heiress Martha Gerry resulted in the production of champions like Nijinsky II, Danzig, Buckpasser, Damascus, Ambiorix, Sir Ivor, Tom Rolfe, Herbager, Forego, and Le Fabuleux. Claiborne Farm was the home of North America's leading sire every year for 15 consecutive years, from 1955 to 1969, while breeding 11 champions in both America and Europe during that period: Doubledogdare, Bayou, Nadir, Round Table, Lamb Chop, Moccasin, Gamely, Wajima, Thatch, Apalachee, and Ivanjica.

The Claiborne tradition continued through Bull Hancock's son, Seth, who famously syndicated Secretariat for $6.02 million (over $40 million today!), and then to Seth's son, Walker Hancock, who was guiding the fortunes of the farm into the decade of the 2020s.

There is little doubt that it was through the insight of Bull Hancock into British and French bloodstock and his recognition of the possibilities they presented that American Thoroughbreds and their pedigrees are the world-wide force they are today. Without the influence of Princequillo, Sir Gallahad, and Nasrullah, the racehorses of today would lack their coveted brilliance.

As the 21st century unfolded, factors like the shrinking globe, currency fluctuations, and specialized equine air transport helped to homogenize and internationalize the racing and breeding world. In the day of Arthur Hancock, Sr., importation of horses was a colossal task, while today's Thoroughbreds travel via aircraft specifically adapted to their needs, and movement of horses for racing and breeding has become an everyday practice. With excessive risk and stress eliminated, trainers like Aidan O'Brien even have been known to ship their runners back home to Ireland between events in North America, Australia, or Asia.

Peter Brant may not have had family roots in racing as deep as the Hancocks. But he was, among his many other fascinating endeavors, known as a household name in the Thoroughbred world beginning in the 1980s. He raced several stakes winners, including champions Waya, Gulch, and Just A Game, and bred 1994 Kentucky Derby and Belmont Stakes winner Thunder Gulch. After taking a twenty-year sabbatical from the game, Brant returned with a flourish in 2016 to race a number of stakes winners, including champion Sistercharlie. In 2018 he purchased Payson Park, one of Florida's premier training facilities, and announced he would be renovating and upgrading both the main track and turf course along with the nearly 500 stalls on the property.

With the advice of respected bloodstock agent Eugenio Colombo, along with the proven success of trainer Chad Brown with grass runners, Brant's approach upon his return to racing was keyed to the importation of quality mares from Ireland, England, and France. In this he was taking a page from Bull Hancock's playbook, but the connection goes deeper than that, for it was Brant's influence in the relocation the 9-year-old stallion Mr. Prospector from Florida to Claiborne Farm in 1979 that led to the establishment of many of the pillars of modern American breeding. Among Mr. Prospector's sons who became influential as stallions have been Gulch, Fappiano, Miswaki, Conquistador Cielo, Machiavellian, Kingmambo, Seeking the Gold, Forty Niner, and Smart Strike.

Any discussion of international racing and breeding would be incomplete without the story of Ireland's Coolmore empire and its development into a global powerhouse from its headquarters in Fethard, County Tipperary.

Coolmore's history begins with Commander Tim Vigors, recipient of the Distinguished Flying Cross for bravery as a fighter pilot with the Royal Air Force in the Battle of Britain during World War II. After the war he worked with the Goffs auction house, then later founded one of the first international bloodstock firms which would eventually become known as the British Bloodstock Agency, Ireland. Upon his father's death, Vigors inherited the family's farm in County Tipperary and developed Coolmore into the original version of the stud farm that exists there today.

Vigors partnered with the Irish trainer Vincent O'Brien, who was already famous in the National Hunt world, having won three consecutive Grand Nationals from 1948-50, before he

Coolmore Stud in Ireland is a breeding showcase.

turned to Thoroughbreds on the flat. To facilitate his transition, O'Brien developed Ballydoyle training center, also in County Tipperary.

Vigors retired, and O'Brien merged his fortunes with John Magnier of Grange Stud, the famous Irish National Hunt stallion center in Fermoy, County Cork. Magnier promptly began the development of the current Coolmore Stud as well as Castlehyde Stud, also in Fermoy, for Thoroughbreds, and continued to breed National Hunt horses at Grange Stud.

Magnier organized a team of backers and investors that included big money principals like soccer pools magnate Robert Sangster, entertainment attorney Danny Schwartz, Greek shipping magnate Stavros Niarchos, and financier Michael Tabor. But it was the moment Magnier brought Sangster into the fold that the course of Coolmore was set. With the team of Vincent O'Brien and his brother, Phonsie, as well as veterinarian Demi O'Byrne, Magnier set out for America with proteges Paul Shanahan and Clem Murphy with the intention of buying the best American-bred yearlings, bringing them back to Ireland, and developing champions to stock the Coolmore stud roster.

It was Vincent O'Brien who insisted that Northern Dancer would be the foundation stone of Coolmore's stallion operation. The Kentucky Derby winner and champion retired to Windfields Farm in Canada in 1965 and then moved to their Maryland location in 1969, never missing a beat in a stunning career at stud. O'Brien and Coolmore focused on Northern Dancer as the principal sire of the sires they expected to develop and stuck with that game plan.

Decades later, you could trace the sire line of every one of the Coolmore stallions to that one horse. From his books of an average of 35 mares – miniscule compared to the stallion bookings of today – Northern Dancer sired not only Sadler's Wells, the titan of Coolmore stallions, but also the outstanding runners and future stallions Danehill, Nijinsky II, Northern Taste, Be My Guest, The Minstrel, Dixieland Band, Fairy King, Vice Regent, Nureyev, and Lyphard.

Coolmore's Galileo, who became the top-rated stallion in the world, was a son of Sadler's Wells whose stud fee for 2019 was what is referred to in the business as "private treaty." In other words, the number was unlisted, but acknowledged to be well above 400,000 euros, or roughly US$500,000. Multiply that by the 200 or so mares each season that would produce one of Galileo's foals, and you can see where the money behind the behemoth organization comes from. Sadly, Galileo passed away in July of 2021 at age 23, due to an injury to a foreleg which refused to heal.

Coolmore's game plan requires that they produce or acquire two or three new stallions of championship, Grade I quality every year in order to move the roster ahead. It also should be noted that the entire Coolmore operation benefited greatly from Ireland's zero tax on stallion fees. Calculated over the first 20 years of the enterprise, that amounted to about $1 billion dollars of tax-free income.

Magnier and his partners devoted the additional income to land purchase and staff development as they expanded to Ashford Stud in Versailles, Ky., and to the 8,000-acre Arrow-field Stud in Australia. The Australian outpost gave Coolmore the option of shuttling select stallions between Northern and Southern Hemisphere to take advantage of the calendar differences in the months associated with breeding seasons.

If nothing else, the Coolmore example vividly illustrates that the use of experts is not taken lightly by the leaders of the sport. Neither should it be taken lightly by investors on a smaller scale. When the Coolmore team goes to the sales, they are accompanied by a legion of trainers, bloodstock agents, business managers, and veterinarians, all playing their part in the selection of potential stallions and mares. Don't expect to compete with them, but certainly try to emulate their professionalism.

Besides Coolmore, there are several other pillars of international bloodstock worth noting, not the least of them is the Darley Stud of Sheikh Mohammed bin Rashid al Maktoum, ruler of Dubai and vice-president of the United Arab Emirates.

Darley stands over 50 stallions at their various global establishments: Dalham Hall Stud in England, Kildangan Stud in Ireland, Jonabell Farm in Kentucky, and Northwood Park and Kelvinside in Australia, as well as stallions at non-Darley farms in Japan and France. In addition, the late Sheikh Hamdan bin Rashid al Maktoum, Mohammed's brother, owned eight stud farms worldwide, most notably in England, Ireland, and Kentucky.

Prince Khalid Abdullah of Saudi Arabia, who died in 2021, was the master of seven stallion stations under his Juddmonte Farms banner: three in England, two in Kentucky, and two in

Ireland. Frankel and Kingman, both European champions, are the leading names among Juddmonte stallions.

For an even deeper dive into the international bloodstock world, I would recommend spending time with Bill Oppenheim's consultancy. Oppenheim's analysis of breeding trends, both in the U.S. and abroad, is an outstanding source of information, especially if you want to compete on a global scale, through his annual review of bloodstock markets and stallion evaluation, with an eye toward potential matings.

The international bloodstock world also embraces Argentina, Uruguay, Chile, Peru, Brazil, and Japan. However, these nations would more commonly be regarded as sources of proven runners which may be integrated into a North American program. It is rare that one would contemplate shipping mares to such destinations for breeding.

Unlike racing in North America, which derives its revenue from a percentage extracted from betting pools known as "takeout," the sport in Europe and South America is principally supported by government subsidy. Although the training fees are lower in those racing nations (approximately 60 percent of U.S. numbers), the purse structure is correspondingly lower, while most other expenses such as veterinary, farrier, dentist, and tack are close to par with the States.

Aside from the Group events that carry six figure purses and a few at a million dollars or more, the prize money structure for ordinary races in European countries is quite low. Winning maidens sometimes earn less than 10,000 of the local currency, whether euros or British pounds.

In Ireland, for example, an EBF (European Breeders Fund) maiden, the equivalent of a U.S. maiden special weight race, might carry a total purse of 12,000-14,000 euros, with only 6,000-8,000 euros going to the winner. A horse of the same ability level in the U.S. would be running for $50,000-80,000.

Purses in England have declined significantly over the past two decades, and other than the top-level events, most handicaps there are equivalent to inexpensive U.S. claimers. Compared to the English model, French racing offers a slightly higher purse scale and more favorable awards for owners and breeders.

There are on-track tote systems at European racetracks, similar to those in the U.S. However, most of the betting in Europe is done through private bookmaking companies, which operate small shops in nearly every town and take wagers on every sport you can imagine. They have a huge internet marketing presence and names like Paddy Power, William Hill, bet365, Ladbrokes, Coral, betWay, uniBet, Betfair, BetVictor, BetFred, QuinnBet, RaceBets, Smarkets, Mr. Green, and 888 Sport. At the tracks, you will find their bookies manning portable pop-up stands on the apron, out-handling the tote system by about 9-to-1. Although the bookies do pay a levy or tax which contributes to the track's operations, it is a drop in the bucket compared to what betting provides the industry in the U.S. and Canada.

Another significant difference between Europe and the rest of the racing world is the Handicap or Rating system. Though a daunting task to assign each horse a specific rating, this system has been an accurate barometer of quality since a professional gambler, racehorse owner and publisher named Phil Bull, issued the first copy of his *Timeform* in 1948. Entitled *Racehorses of 1948*, the publication included a brief description of every horse that raced during the year with a comment on their ability, quality, and temperament, along with an opinion about their chances for improvement.

The *Timeform* philosophy caught on quickly, and eventually a committee was tasked with giving a numerical rating to every horse that competed in the country, publishing the complete list monthly. Although the original publication no longer exists, the system is still used by committees in England,

Ireland, and France to assign a number used to categorize the competition for handicap races, the heart of European racing.

As a personal aside, I have raced horses in Ireland over the past 30 years. And although it is very difficult to show a profit there, the racing culture and the quality of the experience makes it worth the chance. Ireland, a country about the size of Maine, has 26 racetracks that run either flat or jump races every week, although none of them race more than two dozen days in a year. (Maine, by the way, has none.)

The two major Irish tracks are The Curragh and Leopardstown. They were built to accommodate large crowds, and each will host more than 25,000 fans for their biggest days: the Irish Derby run at The Curragh at the end of June and Champions Weekend run at both tracks in in September. The other courses scattered throughout the country make for wonderful day trips. Many conduct evening meets in the summer that begin around 5 p.m. and do not end until after 10, which is not a problem since it stays light until nearly 11.

Laytown, near Ireland's main city of Dublin, races only one day a year. But that day is world famous, with racing conducted on the beach at a vast low tide that attracts more than 10,000 enthusiastic fans who watch from the cliffs above the sand. It should be on every racing fan's bucket list.

Irish racing is administered by an organization called Horse Racing Ireland, which manages registration, silks, entries, jockey and track charges, and purse distribution. Their marketing arm, Irish Thoroughbred Marketing, is an excellent source of information about tracks, trainers, and jockeys.

Racing in the United Kingdom is administered by their version of The Jockey Club, called Weatherbys, under the authority of the British Horseracing Board. They also oversee registration of Irish Thoroughbreds. Similarly, racing in France is administered by an organization called France-Galop.

Should you decide to race in Europe, keep several things in mind. Most trainers there bill monthly, and many will include travel costs and vet expenses at your request. Their percentages for performance are similar to those in the U.S, although fees for licensing, horse naming, and registration of racing colors are charged separately via the individual country's racing organization. These organizations can be most helpful with your stable arrangements, and some will even reimburse travel expenses should you wish to attend auction sales and purchase horses there.

Choose your trainer carefully and check his references, rather than being seduced by a charming accent. Unlike North American racing, horses do not stable and train at the track, but are housed at common training grounds or private facilities, referred to as "yards," from which horses are shipped to the track on their race days. Also, unlike America, trainers for the most part are born into the trade, and most of them own their facilities.

In most European countries, Thoroughbred trainers hold a certain amount of status, like business professionals. During his reign as king of the Europe's trainers, the legendary Vincent O'Brien and his wife Jacqueline held a celebrity similar to the movie stars of the era, she attired in Chanel and Givenchy, he as dapper as William Powell or Clark Gable. That's what comes along with training for royalty and industrial magnates.

Should you decide to give racing in Europe a try, don't be intimidated by the regal settings. Some owners feel that they might not receive the attention they crave if their horse is in a large stable, but those feelings are unfounded. The top trainers there are happy to see a good horse in one of their stalls, no matter who it belongs to, and although they may run three or more horses in some races, they will give preference to the best ones. If your horse isn't up to their standards, believe me, they'll tell you to send it elsewhere, because stalls are at a premium. Lesser trainers may not do so, wishing to keep you around to supplement their daily training rate and help defray their overhead, whether you win races or not. Don't waste your time and money. Go for the best you can get.

Many trainers there are known as "market gardeners" who spend their time readying horses for sale as their principal income. If you end up in one of those stables, expect to hear that your horse will be ready to race in "about two more weeks," and that fortnight may be extended for months before you find out they either can't run or never will, while in fact you've just been contributing to the stable finances and supplementing the trainer's sales program. Once again, this makes the acquisition of a good bloodstock agent/advisor invaluable, as it can be the difference between success and failure ... in any language.

Thoroughbred Investor's Bible

Michael Blowen and one of his retired stars at Old Friends

CHAPTER 12

END GAME

"The greatness of a nation and its moral progress can be judged by how its animals are treated."

~ Mahatma Gandhi

Americans living in the 21st century have become pet oriented to an extraordinary degree. In 2019, more than 100 million U.S. households owned either a dog or a cat, while more than nine million equines were in the domestic herd as companions, performance horses, or backyard pets.

With such widespread animal ownership comes the inevitable issue of their end-of-life care. Most pet owners grapple with the question of how long to care for a sick cat or dog before allowing them to be euthanized under veterinary supervision. The same issues arise for horse owners, along with a history of disposal that has traditionally treated horses as beasts of burden that no longer contribute to the economy.

Racehorses, a luxury item, have been treated in a similar vein. For many years there was a steady pipeline from the bottom levels of racetrack competition to legal slaughterhouses that exported horsemeat to customer nations in Europe and Asia. Itinerant vendors, known as "the killers," would frequent tracks and pay by the pound for horses deemed no longer competitive or injured beyond repair, after which the horses would be resold to a slaughterhouse. Over time, the cruelty and abuses of the horse slaughter industry became so unacceptable to a sufficient majority of Americans that the domestic practice was marginalized, then virtually eliminated through Congressional action, although horses still were victims of export to slaughterhouses in Canada and Mexico.

One of the cold-eyed facts of the racing business is that it's always easier to get a horse than it is to get rid of one, heartless as that sounds. As noted, a well-pedigreed filly may have residual value at the end of her racing career and appeal to a breeder, and buyers find them by the hundreds in the numerous "mixed sales" usually held in the late fall and early winter, while even the most underachieving stallion with a whiff of pedigree may find a stud farm somewhere to call home.

But an unraceable male horse, usually a gelding, may have little or no commercial value at all. And just because a Thoroughbred begins life as a six-figure yearling or two-year-old does not mean he may not end up in claiming races with descending price tags, until he is eventually deemed worthless as even the most modest racing investment. At that point, and with no institutional alternative for retirement, the slaughter option became viable for many owners.

In 1983, New Jersey horse advocate Monique Koehler recognized this serious defect in the Thoroughbred industry and set out to find a solution. Koehler founded the Thoroughbred Retirement Foundation, whose primary purpose was to save racehorses from slaughter.

The TRF and similar organizations fought an uphill battle for years, relying on individual donations and fundraisers to support the horses rescued from slaughter pens or retired directly from racetracks. But it was slow going, and support from major industry organizations was token at best. Then, in 1997, racing fans were shocked to learn that the international

Thoroughbred star Exceller – who defeated Triple Crown winners Seattle Slew and Affirmed in the 1978 Jockey Club Gold Cup – had come to the end of his life in a Swedish slaughterhouse after beginning his stallion career in Kentucky.

Shortly thereafter, the Exceller Foundation was established, with a mission similar to the TRF, and regional organizations began to spring up, offering Thoroughbreds an alternative form of retirement other than slaughter. Then, in 2002, the movement received another traumatic jolt into action when it was reported that 1986 Kentucky Derby winner and 1987 Horse of the Year Ferdinand suffered the same fate as Exceller, this time in a Japanese slaughterhouse. Like Exceller, Ferdinand also began his stallion career in Kentucky before being exported.

In 2008, Suffolk Downs in Boston became the first track in North America to institute a policy whereby any trainer caught knowingly selling a horse for slaughter would be banned from the grounds. Eventually, most tracks adopted a similar policy, but such intentions have been difficult to prove, and the journey of many horses from racetrack to the slaughter pipeline can be hard to trace.

Michael Blowen, retired film critic for the Boston Globe, founded Old Friends Equine near Lexington, Ky., in 2003. The farm has been anchored by a stellar collection of former racing greats – among the residents have been champions Silver Charm, Gulch, Amazombie, Sunshine Forever, and Precisionist – and visitors pay to stroll the farm grounds for a close up look at some of their personal favorites at what is nothing less than a living museum of famous Thoroughbreds. The attraction of the four-legged stars helps support scores of other retired racehorses who were not nearly as famous, sometimes arriving at Old Friends without support from former owners.

Thoroughbreds can have fulfilling lives beyond the racetrack.

"They're all welcome here," Blowen says. "And the blue-collar guys get the same loving care as the champions and Breeders' Cup winners."

Recognizing the need for a unified approach to the problem of caring for racehorses in retirement, in 2012 several major industry organizations – including Breeders' Cup Ltd., The Jockey Club, and Keeneland Association – established and funded the Thoroughbred Aftercare Alliance. The mission of the TAA has been to accredit and help fund the numerous organizations engaged in the rescue, retirement, adoption, retraining, and repurposing of Thoroughbred horses. With support from all corners of the industry, the TAA distributed more than $17 million to accredited organizations in its first seven years of operation and assisted more than 10,000 horses in finding safe haven in retirement.

As a horse owner, you will become aware of a variety of aftercare options and services available. A good place to start is through any local organizations representing owners and trainers. They will know what programs may exist that are funded through the track and/or the horsemen's group, and most of those organizations will have been accredited by the TAA.

If the retired racehorse is healthy and sound, retraining and repurposing present the ideal situation when their racetrack days are over. A sound, healthy Thoroughbred repurposed for a second career will continue to raise up the breed in the after-racing market. There are organizations that specialize in just such conversions, and believe me, a healthy horse is happier if he has a purpose in life beyond nibbling grass and staring at the horizon.

Because of the success of programs such as the Thoroughbred Makeover, Take2, and The Jockey Club's Thoroughbred Incentive Points, Thoroughbreds are now more in demand in the show horse world. There can be some very satisfying results.

One of the most spectacular conversions was the second career enjoyed by a fine racehorse named For the Moment, winner of the 1977 Blue Grass Stakes for trainer LeRoy Jolley. Toward the end of his modest career as a stallion, For the Moment was retrained as a jumper – and he jumped right onto the U.S. Equestrian squad. In 1988, For the Moment could be found at the Summer Olympics in Seoul, South Korea, helping America win a silver medal in team jumping against the world's best.

It would be nice to think every former racehorse at least could be converted into a riding horse for a young boy or girl. But such placement is not always available, and some horses are simply unsuitable for such a new career. Many horses need time off before their retraining can begin. They might not be sound enough to be retrained as a riding horse, and some may lack the right temperament. Such horses are referred to as "pasture sound," still beautiful creatures to behold, but limited in their physical activity. Unfortunately, the placement spots for horses designated as pasture-sound are not as plentiful as needed. They are of proven value in equine-assisted therapeutic programs, but the demand is not as great as the number of retired horses who would be a good fit.

The hard truth is that most horses are raced until they can no longer answer the bell. Hopefully, they are not so physically compromised that their quality of life suffers in retirement, and there are several options for horses that need time off before a second career could be considered.

It always should be a priority to retire your horse to a TAA-accredited, non-profit organization. If your horse needs rehab, you will most likely be required to make a larger donation than if the horse was sound and ready for retraining. One way or the other, you can be confident the horse is enjoying retirement at such a facility, and you can check on him regularly while continuing your support.

"Placing a horse in a sanctuary home may take some time," said Erin Shea of the TAA. "Many equine sanctuaries have large, aging herds, so patience and clear communication of your horse's needs are key to re-homing your horse. Also, just because a horse cannot be a competitive athlete does not mean that they cannot have a new career. For example, TAA-accredited organizations Saratoga War Horse, Equine Rescue of Aiken, Life Horse at Breezy Hill, and Square Peg, among others, all focus on equine-human therapy along with sanctuary for horses."

The Second Chances Program of the Thoroughbred Retirement Foundation maintains pasture-sound horses at prison-based farms where the horses have a meaningful second career rehabilitating incarcerated men and women.

A second alternative is retirement boarding. The cost will be approximately $200 to $500 per month, not including hoof trimming (which averages $40 every eight weeks) and vet care (vaccinations and teeth care run an average of $350 per year). Retirement boarding farms now exist all over the U.S., and as the primary person of support, you have control over the horse's well-being.

As a third option, you could choose to sell or give your horse away. But care must be taken. No one wants their horse to end up in the kill pen, bound for a slaughterhouse in Canada or Mexico. Besides, most tracks have a policy which states that any horse owner or trainer found to have directly or indirectly sold a horse that ends up in the slaughter pipeline will have their stalls permanently revoked. This could happen unknowingly if you are not careful about vetting out the buyer or recipient.

Diana Pikulski, former executive director of the Thoroughbred Retirement Foundation and currently the editor of the Thoroughbred Adoption Network, offers the following tips to help ensure your horse's safety if you give them away, or sell at a giveaway price:

--Use a signed agreement like the one provided by CANTER USA to the trainers who chose to list horses for sale on its website.

--Consider a "first right of refusal" clause requiring the buyer to agree that they will not give away or sell the horse without first asking if you want it back.

--Consider a clause that allows for you to check on the horse.

--Obtain a copy of the buyer's driver's license.

--Include in sales agreement language that the buyer will never put the horse in a livestock auction or sell it to slaughter buyers.

--Have the agreement notarized.

--Require a professional reference from a veterinarian. Ask the vet when they last visited the farm where your horse is heading or witnessed the condition and care of the horses owned by the person buying your horse. Obtain the veterinarian's license number.

--Sell the horse as "Retired from Racing" and execute the appropriate forms provided by The Jockey Club.

"Thoroughbreds are more in demand as riding horses than ever in the past 30 or so years, thanks in large part to incentive programs like TIP and Take2, as well as the work of Retired Racehorse Project," says Nancy Koch, Executive Director of CANTER, USA. "But owners and trainers must use due diligence in their transactions. It is extremely important to get references and check on the horse or have someone check on the horse a week or so after it leaves to be sure it is adjusting, and the people are who they represented themselves to be."

(A complete list of those organizations accredited by the Thoroughbred Aftercare Alliance can be found in Appendix 6.)

Being part of an ownership syndicate adds a few issues for owners seeking to secure a second career or retirement for a racehorse. Regina Schneller, an owner who is active in racing partnerships, has her name and address attached to all the official papers accompanying the horses in the partnerships, in the event one is claimed and is owned by someone else at the time of retirement.

"To find homes, the first thing that our partnership does is ask if any partners are interested in giving the horse a home," Schneller said. "If the horse has problems, then I make take the horse or board it at a retirement farm. I then ask the other partners to chip in on the board/donation. One horse recently needed a period of time to be turned out before training, so he went to CANTER, and I paid for his care until he was ready to be adopted."

It may seem counterproductive to think in terms of the end of an investment adventure at the very beginning. But Thoroughbreds are creatures who need care throughout their lives, and on average they live to be 20, far past their racing years. Ownership can be spread through many hands – from breeding to selling to buying to claiming to standing at stud. At some point, someone needs to step up and fulfill the obligation to their aftercare. Fortunately, there are a growing number of organizations and funding mechanisms to provide owners with safe, responsible options.

The author – always ready for the winner's circle

AFTERWORD

My father wasn't one to dispense advice easily, but when he did, I usually listened. Not necessarily followed the advice but listened. One of his admonitions could be described as a cliché, since it was heard often as many fathers passed it on: "Do something you love, and you'll never have to work a day in your life."

I think he was hoping my passions would lead me to a life of service to others, following him into the world of medicine. Instead, I signed on at the racetrack and never looked back.

Although not a good student, I did find an entrancing world in literature and spent plenty of my time reading. Joe Palmer, Grantland Rice, and Red Smith whetted my appetite for sports, Damon Runyon for gambling tales, and the writing of Bill Nack, Ed Pope, and Joe Hirsch inspired dreams that someday I might join their fraternity.

That did not happen either. It was the racetrack itself that called, and as the years rolled by, I did have the good fortune to work alongside many of the characters immortalized by Hirsch, Nack, and my other literary idols. During my career as a jockey agent, I rubbed elbows with Secretariat's trainer and worked with several Kentucky Derby winning jockeys, as well as a multitude of Hollywood celebrities. I had the opportunity to build farms and training facilities, breed champion racehorses, and have my picture taken in many a winner's circle. My world became the Grandstand, the Clubhouse, and the grounds of America's endlessly diverse racetracks, both large and small, and more importantly their stable areas, wherein beats the heart of the sport.

The space required for my thank you list would call for another dozen pages, so I'll make this a blanket bow to all the hotwalkers, grooms, and exercise folks, jockeys and agents, trainers and owners, track administrators and officials, and especially the talented people who made me look good for so many years. Oh, and the gamblers and grifters, too, as well as David Milch, the living, breathing personification of my glorious racing world.

I survived, sometimes even thrived, and in so doing I proved my old man right from the start. In a lifetime at the racetrack, I have never "worked" a day. Hopefully, some of the lessons learned in that lifetime will come through in your *Thoroughbred Investor's Bible* – call it a catechism, a guide book, a collection of proven recipes – enabling and fueling your newly found passion to become a part of the greatest game played outdoors.

--J.P.

APPENDICES

Appendix #1

ANNUAL NORTH AMERICAN REGISTERED FOAL CROP

Year	U.S. (% change)	Canada	Puerto Rico	Total (%change)
1990	40,333 (-8.2)	3,193	617	44,143 (-7.5)
1991	38,151 (-5.4)	3,025	628	41,804 (-5.3)
1992	35,051 (-8.1)	2,777	610	38,438 (-8.1)
1993	33,822 (-3.5)	2,713	605	37,140 (-3.4)
1994	32,118 (-5.0)	2,591	632	35,341 (-4.8)
1995	31,884 (-0.7)	2,446	653	34,983 (-1.0)
1996	32,243 (1.1)	2,397	726	35,366 (1.1)
1998	32,947 (2.6)	2,340	734	36,021 (2.5)
1999	33,844 (2.7)	2,435	650	36,929 (2.5)
2000	34,728 (2.6)	2,465	562	37,755 (2.2)
2001	34,721 (-0.0)	2,590	590	37,901 (0.4)
2002	32,986 (-5.0)	2,468	524	35,978 (-5.1)
2003	33,976 (3.0)	2,576	515	37,067 (3.0)
2004	34,800 (2.4)	2,615	534	37,949 (2.4)
2005	35,050 (0.7)	2,788	527	38,365 (1.1)
2006	34,905 (-0.4)	2,643	556	38,104 (-0.7)
2007	34,358 (-1.6)	2,546	595	37,499 (-1.6)
2008	32,332 (-5.9)	2,382	560	35,274 (-5.9)
2009	29,612 (-8.4)	2,323	429	32,364 (-8.2)
2010	25,954 (-12.4)	2,118	347	28,419 (-12.2)
2011	22,653 (-12.7)	1,991	295	24,939 (-12.2)
2012	21,469 (-5.2)	1,782	290	23,541 (-5.6)
2013	21,429 (-0.2)	1,533	284	23,246 (-1.3)
2014	21,418 (-0.1)	1,287	287	22,992 (-1.1)
2015	21,486 (0.3)	1,301	217	23,004 (0.1)
2016	21,024 (-2.2)	1,321	227	22,572 (1.9)
2017	20,656 (-0.6)	1,362	221	22,239 (-0.3)
2018	19,717 (-4.7)	1,320	204	21,500 (-4.4)
2019	19.295 (-2.1)*	1,275*	230*	20,800 (-2.1)*
2020	19,010 (-1.5)*	1,275*	215*	20,500 (-1.4)*

* Estimated figures   Source: The Jockey Club

Appendix #2

NATIONAL RACING COMPACT
(Table of licensing fees)

	Owner	TB Trainer	Harness Trainer	Jockey	Driver	Stable	Partnership	Colors
Arizona	$150	$150		$200		$150		
Arkansas	$60	$55		$55		$60	$60	
California (3-year)	$150	$150	$150	$150	$150	$300	$300	
Delaware (Harness)	$50		$50		$50			
Delaware (TB)	$50	$50		$30		$25	$25	
Delaware (TB) 3 -Year	$150	$150		$90		$75	$75	
Florida (3-year)	$80	$80	$80	$80	$80	$120	$120	
Illinois	$25	$25		$25		$50 **	$25	
Illinois (Harness)	$25		$25		$25	USTAreg	USTAreg	
Indiana	$35							
Iowa (2 year)	$10	$10	$10	$10	$10	$10	$10	
Kentucky (Throughbred)	$150	$150		$150				
Kentucky (Harness)	$125		$125		$125			
Louisiana	$25	$25		$35		$50	$25	$25
Louisiana (3-year)	$75	$75		$105				$75
Maryland (Throughbred)	100*	100*		Free		Free	Free	
Maryland (Harness)	Free		Free		Free	Free		
Massachusetts	$30	$30	$30			$60	$50	
Michigan	$25	$25	$25	$25	$25	$10	$10	
Minnesota	$50							
Nebraska	Free	Free		Free		$50	$15	
New Mexico	$120	$120				$120		
New Mexico (3-year)	$220	$220				$220		
New Jersey	$50	$50	$50			$50	$50	
New Jersey (3-year)	$150							
New York (New)	$175	$105	$95	$136.50	$106.50			
New York (New 2-year)	$225	$165	$145	$186.50	$126.50			
New York (New 3-year)	$275	$215	$195	$236.50	$146.50			
New York (Renewal)	$50	$30	$20	$50	$20			
New York (Renewal - 2-year)	$100	$60	$40	$100	$40			
New York (Renewal - 3-year)	$150	$90	$60	$150	$60			
Ohio	$50			$50		$25**	$25	
Oklahoma	$50	$50		$50		$10	$10	
Oklahoma (3-year)	$120	$120		$120				
Pennsylvania (Standardbred)	$120							
Pennsylvania (TB - 3-year)	$120					$60	$60	$15
Texas	$100	$100		$100		$35	$35	
Texas (2-year)	$200	$200		$200		$70	$70	
Texas (3-year)	$300	$300		$300		$105	$105	
Virginia (2-year)	$0	$0	$0	$0	$0	$0		
Washington	$246*	$83		$83		$59		
West Virginia	$30	$30		$30		$40		
Wyoming	$35	$35		$35		$35		

Appendix #3

JOCKEY CLUB NAMING RULES

--A name may be claimed on the Registration Application, on a Name Claiming Form or through Interactive Registration TM at www.registry.jockeyclub.com. Name selections should be listed in order of preference. Names will be assigned based upon availability and compliance with the naming rules as stated herein. Names may not be claimed or reserved by telephone. When a foreign language name is submitted, an English translation must be furnished to The Jockey Club. An explanation must accompany "coined" or "made-up" names that have no apparent meaning. Horses that were born in the United States, Puerto Rico or Canada and currently reside in another country must be named by The Jockey Club through the Stud Book Authority of their country of residence.

--If a valid attempt to name a foal is submitted to The Jockey Club by February 1 of the foal's two-year-old year and such a name is determined not eligible for use, no fee is required for a subsequent claim of name for that foal. If a valid attempt to name a foal is not submitted to The Jockey Club by February 1 of the foal's two-year-old year, a fee is required to claim a name for such a foal (see Fee Schedule).

--A reserved name must be used within one year from the day it was reserved. Reserved names cannot be used until notification requesting the assignment of the name to a specific horse is received by the Registry Office. If the reserved name is not used within one year from its reservation, it will become available for any horse. A fee is required to reserve a name (see Fee Schedule).

--A foal's name may be changed at any time prior to starting in its first race. Ordinarily, no name change will be permitted after a horse has started in its first race or has been used for breeding purposes. However, in the event a name must be changed after a horse has started in its first race, both the old and new names should be used until the horse has raced three times following the name change. The prescribed fee (see Fee Schedule) and the Certificate of Foal Registration must accompany any request to the Registry Office for a change of name.

--Names of horses over ten years old may be eligible for use if they are not excluded under Rule 6(F) and have not been used during the preceding five years either for breeding or racing.

--Names of horses that were never used for breeding or racing may be available for use five years from the date of their death as reported.

The following classes of names are not eligible for use:

--Names consisting of more than 18 letters (spaces and punctuation marks count as letters).

--Names consisting entirely of initials such as C.O.D., F.O.B., etc.

--Names ending in "filly," "colt," "stud," "mare," "stallion," or any similar horse-related term.

--Names consisting entirely of numbers. Numbers above thirty may be used if they are spelled out.

--Names ending with a numerical designation such as "2nd" or "3rd," whether or not such a designation is spelled out.

--Names of living persons unless written permission to use their name is on file with The Jockey Club.

--Names of persons no longer living unless approval is granted by The Jockey Club based upon a satisfactory written explanation submitted to the Registrar.

--Names of racetracks or graded stakes races.

--Names clearly having commercial, artistic, or creative significance.

--Names that are suggestive or have a vulgar or obscene meaning; names considered in poor taste; or names that may be offensive to religious, political, or ethnic groups.

--Names that appear to be designed to harass, humiliate, or disparage a specific individual, group of individuals or entity.

--Names that are currently active either in racing or breeding.

- Names of winners in the past 25 years of Grade I stakes races.

Also, you may not use a name designated as "permanent," which includes the following:

--Horses in racing's Hall of Fame;

--Horses that have been voted Horse of the Year;

--Horses that have won an Eclipse Award;

--Horses that have won a Sovereign Award (Canadian Champions);

--Annual leading sire and broodmare sire by progeny earnings;

--Cumulative money winners of $2 million or more;

--Horses that have won the Kentucky Derby, Preakness, Belmont Stakes, The Jockey Club Gold Cup, the Breeders' Cup Classic, or the Breeders' Cup Turf; and

--Horses included in the International List of Protected Names.

--Names similar in spelling or pronunciation to the classes of names listed above.

--Names of horses previously recorded in The American Stud Book by the same sire or out of the same dam as the foal for which the attempt is made.

--Names of horses appearing within the first five generations of the pedigree of the foal for which the attempt is made.

Appendix #4

JOCKEY CLUB COLORS RULES
(Enforced in New York only)

1. Front and back of silks must be identical, except for seam design.
2. Colors must be registered in the name of one person only; NOT a stable name or Mr. & Mrs. (example: Mary E. Jones).
3. Designs are limited to those on the reverse side of this form.
4. Navy blue is NOT an available color.
5. A maximum of two colors is allowed on the jacket and two on the sleeves for a maximum of four colors.
6. These colors will be renewable on December 31st of the year they are registered.
7. You may have an acceptable emblem or up to three initials on the ball, yoke, circle, or braces design. You may have one initial on the opposite shoulder of the sash design, the box frame, or the diamond.

Appendix #5

THOROUGHBRED SYNDICATES

(Nationally ranked or those with approximately 40 starts and earnings in excess of $250,000 in 2021)

Bourbon Lane Stable (Racing)
Midway, KY
www.Mcmahonandhill.com

Bradley Thoroughbreds (Racing/Breeding)
Lexington, KY
www.bradleythoroughbreds.com

Bush Racing Stable (Claiming)
Grantville, PA
www.bushracingstable.com

Centennial Farms (Racing/Breeding)
Beverly, MA
www.centennialfarms.com

Country Life Farm (Racing/Breeding)
Fallston, MD
www.countrylifefarm.com

Dare to Dream Stable (Racing/Claiming)
Gurnee, IL
www.daretodreamstable.com

Donegal Racing (Racing)
Des Moines, IO
www.donegalracing.com

Drawing Away Stable (Racing)
New York, NY
www.nyrainc.com

Eclipse Thoroughbred Partners (Racing)
Augusta, SC
www.eclipsetbpartners.com

Hibiscus Stables (Racing/Claiming)
Mahopac, NY
www.hibiscusstables.com

Horseplayers Racing Club (Racing)
Renton, WA
www.horseplayersracingclub.com

Iron Horse Racing Stable (Racing)
New York, NY
www.ihracing.com

It's All About the Girls Racing (Racing/Breeding)
Lexington, KY
www.itsallaboutthegirlsracing.com

Kenwood Racing (Racing)
Oceanport, NJ
www.kenwoodracing.com

Lady Sheila Stable (Racing/Breeding)
Hyde Park, NY
www.ladysheilastabletwo.com

Little Red Feather Racing (Racing)
Woodland Hills, CA
www.littleredfeather.com

Magdalena Racing (Racing)
Lexington, KY
www.magdelenaracing.com

Pewter Racing Stable (Racing)
Mullica Hill, NJ
www.pewterstable.com

Pocket Aces Racing (Racing)
Lexington, KY
www.pocketacesracing.com

Shooting Star Thoroughbreds (Racing)
Williston, FL
www.shootingstartb.com

Starlight Racing (Racing)
Lexington, KY
www.starlightracing.com

Team Valor International (Racing/Breeding)
Lake Worth, FL
www.teamvalor.com

Ten Strike Racing (Racing)
Oaklawn Park, AK
www.tenstrikeracing.com

Twin Creeks Racing (Racing)
Versailles, KY
www.twincreeksracing.com

Uptowncharlybrown Stud (Racing)
Parx, PA
www.utcbstud.com

West Point Thoroughbreds (Racing/Breeding)
Saratoga Springs, NY
www.westpointtb.com

Woodford Racing (Racing/Breeding)
Versailles, KY
www.woodfordracing.com

Appendix #6

TAA APPROVED AFTERCARE ORGANIZATIONS

List provided by the Thoroughbred Aftercare Alliance.
Websites, addresses, etc., for individual organizations available at
www.thoroughbredaftercarealliance.org

Arizona
After the Homestretch
Equine Encore Foundation
Harmony and Hope Horse Haven

British Columbia
New Stride Thoroughbred Adoption Society

California
CANTER California
Forever Free Horse Rescue
Glen Ellen Vocational Academy (GEVA)
Healing Arenas
Heaven Can Wait
Hope for Horses Inc.
Horse Power Sanctuaries dba Redwings Horse Sanctuary
Humanity for Horses
Los Angeles Pet Rescue/Farralone Farms
Neigh Savers Foundation
Redwings Horse Sanctuary
Saving Horses
Southern California Thoroughbred Rescue
Square Peg Foundation
Thoroughbred Rehab Center
Training Racehorses off the Track (TROTT)
Tranquility Farm
United Pegasus Foundation
White Rock Ranch Horse Rescue and Retirement
Win Place Home

Colorado
CANTER Colorado

Connecticut
Mitchell Farm Equine Retirement
Racing For Home

Florida
Diamonds in the Rough Farm
Equestrian Inc.
Equine Rescue & Adoption Foundation
Final Furlong
Florida Thoroughbred Retirement and Adoptive Care Program (TRAC)
Hidden Acres Rescue for Thoroughbreds
Peaceful Ridge Rescue
RVR Horse Rescue
South Florida SPCA
Thoroughbred Retirement of Tampa Inc.

Illinois
Galloping Out
Illinois Equine Humane Center

Indiana
Friends of Ferdinand

Iowa
Hope After Racing Thoroughbreds (HART)

Kentucky
Blue Horse Charities
CANTER Kentucky
Central Kentucky Riding for Hope
Exceller Fund
Kentucky Equine Adoption Center
Kentucky Equine Humane Center
Kentucky Horse Park Foundation
Maker's Mark Secretariat Center
New Vocations Racehorse Adoption
Old Friends
Our Mims Retirement Haven

Second Stride
Susan S. Donaldson Foundation
The Exceller Fund
Thoroughbred Incentive Program (TIP)

Louisiana
Thoroughbred Retirement Network of Louisiana

Maryland
After the Races
Days End Farm
Foxie G Foundation
Life Horse Inc.
Mid-Atlantic Horse Rescue
Retired Racehorse Project
Thoroughbred Placement Resources

Michigan
Beyond the Roses Equine Rescue and Retirement
CANTER Michigan
Out Side In

Minnesota
This Old Horse, Inc - Racehorse Reimagined

New Jersey
New Beginnings
Second Call Thoroughbreds
South Jersey Thoroughbred Rescue

New Mexico
Harmony and Hope Horse Haven Inc.

New York
ACTT Naturally
Akindale Thoroughbred Rescue
Equine Advocates Inc.
Finger Lakes Thoroughbred Adoption Program
Lollypop Farm
Lucky Orphans Horse Rescue
ReRun Inc.
Saratoga Warhorse Foundation

Second Chance Thoroughbreds
Take2 Second Career Thoroughbred Program
Thoroughbred Retirement Foundation (TRF)

North Carolina
Blue Bloods Thoroughbred Adoption and Placement

North Dakota
Bowman Second Chance Thoroughbred Adoption

Ohio
CANTER Ohio
New Vocations Racehorse Adoption Program

Oklahoma
Horse and Hound Rescue Foundation
Oklahoma Thoroughbred Retirement Program
Thoroughbred Athletes

Ontario
LongRun Thoroughbred Retirement Society

Pennsylvania
After the Races
Bright Futures Farm
R.A.C.E. Fund Inc.

Puerto Rico
Caribbean Thoroughbred Aftercare

South Carolina
Equine Rescue of Aiken

Texas
Lonestar Outreach to Place Ex-Racers (LOPE)
Remember Me Rescue

Vermont
AFTER the Track

Virginia
Brook Hill Retirement Center for Horses Inc.

Hope's Legacy Equine Rescue
Second Wind Thoroughbred Project
War Horses at Rose Bower

Washington
Center for Racehorse Retraining
Down the Stretch Ranch

West Virginia
Heart of Phoenix Equine Rescue

Wisconsin
Amazing Grace Equine Sanctuary

Appendix #7

RECOMMENDED WEBSITES

GENERAL
www.jockeyclub.com North America's custodian of rules and regulations
www.equibase.com Statistics, Past Performances
www.toba.org Thoroughbred Owners and Breeders Association
www.salesintegrity.org TOBA's sales integrity task force
www.ntra.com The National Thoroughbred Racing Association
www.ntwo.org National advocates for the horse
www.americasbestracing.net Thoroughbred industry marketing
www.thoroughbredracingassociations.com Home of TRPB, Equibase
www.tha.com Thoroughbred Horsemen's Association – Affiliated State horsemen's groups
www.consignorsandbreeders.com Consignor's and Commercial Breeders Association
www.ownerview.com Collaborative site of The Jockey Club and TOBA, specific to ownership
www.horsecouncil.org American Horse council - resource for information on all breeds
www.trpb.com Thoroughbred Racing Protective Bureau

INFORMATION SOURCES
www.stevebyk.com At the Races with Steve Byk on Sirius/XM - Live daily racing radio
www.bloodhorse.com BloodHorse - Industry news and link to *The Source*
www.brisnet.com Brisnet - Past performances, handicapping, and pedigree research
www.drf.com Daily Racing Form – Traditional industry publication
www.horseracingnation.com Horse Racing Nation - Daily news and racing information
www.racingmuseum.com National Museum of Racing – Racing museum and Hall of Fame
www.racingpost.com Racing Post - Europe's version of *Daily Racing Form*
www.paulickreport.com The Paulick Report – Aggregated and original industry reporting
www.thetdn.com Thoroughbred Daily News - Comprehensive and insightful news site
www.tbheritage.com Thoroughbred Heritage - Repository of historical racing information
www.thoroughbredracing.com Thoroughbred Racing Commentary - Features & commentary
www.kentuckypress.com University of Kentucky Press - Racing related books

LEGAL/ACCOUNTING
www.bushlawoffices.com Bing Bush. Based in California and Kentucky
www.brewsterlaw.com Clark Brewster. Based in Oklahoma
www.greenco.com Len Green Accounting. Based in New Jersey
www.horselaw.com Mike Meuser. Based in Kentucky
www.andrewmollicalaw.com Andrew Mollica. Based in New York
www.thoroughbrelaw.com Darrell Vienna. Based in California

PEDIGREES/HEALTH
www.werkhorse.com Pedigree consulting
www.pedigreeconsultants.com Pedigree consulting
www.truenicks.com Pedigree consulting
www.thehorse.com Guide to equine health
www.pedigreequery.com Free pedigree listings

INTERNATIONAL
www.weatherbys.co.uk Europe's custodian of racing rules and regulations
www.ifhaonline.com International racing resources
www.thoroughbred-businessguide.com European based, 7,000 industry contacts
www.hri.ie Horse Racing Ireland – industry administration
www.racehorseownership.ie Irish racing information
www.itm.ie Irish Thoroughbred Marketing
www.attheraces.com Euro-link to all things racing. Entries, results, and betting sites
www.theirishfield.ie Daily trade paper of Irish horse racing
www.breedingracing.com Australia and New Zealand racing

HORSE SALES
www.fasigtipton.com Auctions in KY, FL, Saratoga
www.keeneland.com World's largest venue of equine auctions
www.obs.com Florida auction venue
www.goffs.com Goffs auction company, Ireland
www.goffsuk.com Goffs auction company, UK
www.tatersalls.com Tattersalls – Europe's leading bloodstock auction house
www.inglis.com.au Inglis – Australia's leading bloodstock auction house
www.arquana.com French equine auctions

RETIREMENT/REPURPOSING
www.thoroughbredaftercare.org Accreditation body for aftercare organizations
www.tca.com Thoroughbred Charities of America
www.Take2tbreds.com – 2nd careers
www.tbmakeover.com Retirement
www.sctap.com Adoption and placement

WAGERING/ADW/REPLAY SITES
(sources of streaming live racing)
www.XpressBet.com 1 S/T tracks
www.Tvg.com General
www.Twinspires.com Churchill/CDI
www.Nyrabets.com New York Racing Assoc.
www.rtn.tv Roberts Racing Television Network

GLOSSARY
OF THOROUGHBRED TERMS

A

ACE OR ACEPROMAZINE – Standard tranquilizer for horses, used principally for nervous horses when vanning or in other situations when a horse may become agitated such as shoeing, dental work or hair clipping.

ADDED MONEY – Funds added to the amount paid by owners, contributed to purses by the track for stakes races.

ALLOWANCE RACE – An event other than a claiming race for which the Racing Secretary specifies certain conditions for eligibility and weighting.

ALLOWANCES – Weight or other conditions for a race.

ALSO-ELIGIBLE – A horse entered but not permitted to run unless the size of the field is reduced to a specific number by scratches.

ALSO RAN – A horse that finished out of the money, traditionally lower than win, place, or show.

ANKLE – That part of the leg of a horse between the cannon and pastern, also called the fetlock.

ANKLE BOOT -- A rubber protective covering worn over the fetlock.

APPRENTICE JOCKEY – A rider of relative inexperience who is allowed a weight concession of from five to 10 pounds depending on how many winners they have recorded, as indicated in the program by asterisks, thus the term "bug rider."

ASSISTANT STARTER – Employees of the track whose job it is to help load the horses into the starting gate.

AT THE POST – When the horses reach the gate, but are not yet in the gate.

B

BABY RACE -- A race for two-year-olds.

BACKSIDE – The stable area.

BACKSTRETCH – The straight part of the track on the far side between turns; slang term referring to the stable area.

BAD ACTOR – An unwilling, hard to handle or tough horse.

BADGE LIST – A trainer's list registered with the Racing Secretary which includes all horses, owners, and employees.

BALD or BALD-FACED – A horse with a white face.

BALL – Oral medication, usually a physic, administered by a "balling gun," similar to a dose syringe.

BANDAGE – Long strips of cloth wound around the lower part of horse's legs for support or protection, either in the stall or during a race. Also called brace, standing, or polo bandages.

BAR SHOE – A special horseshoe on which the heels are connected by a bar, designed to keep the hoof from spreading. Normally used when a horse has foot problems such as a quarter crack.

BARREL – The round part of a horse's body between the forequarters and hindquarters.

BARREN – A mare which has failed to conceive.

BARRIER – The starting gate or other method used to start a race.

BATTERY – An illegal, hand-held electrical device used by a rider to make a horse run faster.

BAY – Horse color, varying from light tan to dark brown, with black mane and tail.

BILL DALY – A horse sent to the lead is said to be "on the Bill Daly," in reference to a colorful trainer of the 1800s who taught his riders in that style.

BIT – Any of the many variations of the metal bar in a horse's mouth that enable the rider to guide and control the animal with reins.

BLACKSMITH – The person who shoes horses, also known as a farrier or plater.

BLACK TYPE – The boldface type in a catalog style pedigree for horses that have won or placed in a stakes race. Boldface caps indicate a stakes winner, lower case indicates stakes-placed.

BLANKET FINISH – A group of horses close together at the wire.

BLEEDER – A horse that displays traces of blood from their lungs because of Exercise Induced Pulmonary Hemorrhaging (EIPH), which is measured in degrees of severity on a one-to-five scale.

BLINKERS – AKA blinders, a hood with eye-cups designed to limit a horse's peripheral vision.

BLIND SWITCH – When a horse is trapped in a pocket and has nowhere to go.

BLISTER – A caustic irritant applied to a horse's leg in order to increase blood flow and promote healing.

BLOCK HEEL – A type of racing shoe or plate raised at the back to prevent a horse from "running down," i.e. rubbing the heels raw.

BLOODLINE – The pedigree of a horse.

BLOODSTOCK – Thoroughbred horses.

BLOODSTOCK AGENT – A broker who represents sellers or buyers of Thoroughbred horses.

BLOW THE TURN – A horse that runs wide on the bend.

BOG SPAVIN – An inflammation of the hock joint (hind leg) caused by strain and indicated by puffiness and swelling.

BOLT – A horse that suddenly veers to the outside.

BONE SPAVIN – A bony growth inside and at the front of the hock, caused by strain.

BOTTOM LINE – The female side of a Thoroughbred's family.

BOWED TENDON – An injury caused by a strain of the superficial flexor tendon located below the knee or hock. Requires a long period of rehabilitation and may be career ending.

BREAKING – Training the young Thoroughbred to accept a rider on a saddle, usually done in the fall of the horse's yearling year.

BREAK MAIDEN – When a horse or jockey wins their first race.

BREAK ON TOP - When a horse leaves the starting gate in front.

BRED - Referring to the location of a horse at the time of birth. Also refers to the act of mating.

BREEDER - The owner of the mother of a foal at the time it is born.

BREEDING RIGHT - The entitlement to breed one mare to a stallion for one or more breeding seasons.

BREEZE - A horse's workout at near racing speed.

BRIDLE - Headgear for the horse used to control and steer it.

BROODMARE - A female horse used for breeding.

BROODMARE SIRE - The sire of a Thoroughbred's dam. Also refers to a stallion known to sire productive daughters.

BRUSHING - An injury to the fetlock caused by a strike from the opposite foot.

BULLET - The fastest work of the day for a given distance, as indicated by a black dot on workout reports.

BULL RING - A small racetrack, usually five or six furlongs in circumference.

BUSH TRACK - A minor racetrack, sometimes illegal or unauthorized.

BUTE - Short for the product Butazolidin (generic phenylbutazone), a commonly used non-steroidal anti-inflammatory, legal within certain limits in most jurisdictions.

C

CALF-KNEED - A horse whose forelegs bend back at the knees. Also referred to as "back at the knee."

CALK - A racing shoe with extensions on the bottom to give more traction, usually called a mud calk.

CANNON - The bone on a horse's foreleg between the knee and the ankle; on the hind leg between the hock and the ankle.

CANTER - A slow gallop.

CANTLE - The back of a saddle.

CAPPED HOCK - A swelling on the hock of a horse due to an injury.

CAST - When a horse is unable to get up in their stall.

CHALK - A horse favored in the betting.

CHANGE LEADS - When a horse alternates from leading with one foot or the other in the stride cycle.

CHECK - When the rider is forced to alter course or slow a horse during a race.

CHESTNUT - Copper horse color varying from dark liver to light yellow. Also, the name for the small, callus-like growths on the inside of a horse's legs.

CHOPPY - A short, awkward stride, often indicating soreness or unsoundness.

CHUTE -- A straight extension of the racing strip leading to the main course, enabling races to avoid starting on a turn.

CIRCUIT - A group of race tracks in any geographical region on which horsemen compete, usually with consecutive racing dates.

CLAIMING RACE - A race in which each horse entered is eligible to be purchased at a set price, with the funds committed via a signed claim slip before the race begins.

CLAIM BOX - A receptacle in which the claim slip is placed.

211

CLERK OF SCALES – The official whose principal duty is to weigh the jockeys before and after a race to ensure that the proper weight is carried.

CLOCKER – A person who times the horses during morning workouts. They may work for the track, the Daily Racing Form/Equibase, or privately.

CLUBHOUSE TURN – The first turn past the finish line, where the Club House is commonly located.

COGGINS TEST – A test for Equine Infectious Anemia (EIA) or swamp fever, required for a horse to enter a track's stable area.

COLORS – An owner's individual racing silks worn by jockeys, unique and registered with the jurisdiction's administrative body.

COLT – A male horse other than a gelding or ridgling which has not reached its fifth birthday, after which it is referred to as a horse.

COLD WATER BANDAGES – Bandages that have been soaked in ice water before application, in order to minimize inflammation in the horse's shins.

COLIC – Digestive tract disorder in the horse that can range from mild to life-threatening.

CONDITION BOOK – A publication produced by the Racing Secretary listing all the races to be offered, usually over a period of ten days to two weeks. It is used by trainers to decide in which race to enter, based on the horse's eligibility.

CONFORMATION – The physical structure of a horse.

COOLER – A light blanket or sheet placed over a horse after a race or workout while they are walked while returning to normal body temperature.

COOLING OUT – Walking the horse while after exercise, usually around 30-40 minutes.

COUPLED – Two or more horses running as a single betting unit, also called an entry, due to their having a common ownership.

COVER – A term used for the act of breeding a mare by a stallion. The cover date referred to in a sales catalog is the last time that mare was bred in that season.

COW HOCKS – When a horse's hocks are turned inward, similar to a cow's.

CROSS – The manner in which a jockey holds the reins, with one crossing over the other.

CROUP – The upper part of a horse's hindquarters from the loins to the base of the tail.

CRYPTORCHID – A male horse whose testicles have not descended from his abdomen to his scrotum. If one testicle is down, the horse is referred to as a ridgling.

CRIBBER – A horse who grabs an object like a fence or stall door with its teeth and swallows air. Also known as a wind-sucker.

CURB – A swelling and thickening of ligaments around the lower part of the hock.

CUT – A colloquial expression for castration.

D

DAM – A broodmare, or the mother of a horse. The "first dam" is the mother of a horse, the second dam is the first dam's mother, etc.

DAY MONEY - The daily fee that a trainer charges to maintain a horse.

DEAD HEAT – Two or more horses reaching the finish line at exactly the same time.

DERBY – A stakes race exclusively for three-year-olds.

DETENTION BARN – A facility designated for taking blood or urine tests, either pre- or post-race.

DISTAFF – Referring to the female horse or, more specifically, the female side of a horse's family.

DISTANCE OF GROUND – Refers to races over a mile.

DOGS – Traffic cones or barriers placed on a track to prevent horses from exercising along the inner rail, usually when conditions are muddy.

DOUBLE CALL – When a jockey is named on more than one horse in a race.

DWELT – When a horse fails to break when the gate opens.

E

EIGHTH – The common unit of measure designating an eighth of a mile, or 220 yards, called a "furlong" in racing parlance.

ENTRANCE FEE – Monies paid by the owner of a horse to participate in a stakes race.

ENTRY – Two or more horses owned by the same entity, coupled in a race for betting purposes.

ENTRY CLERK – An employee of the track responsible for accepting entries.

EXCUSED – A horse allowed by the stewards to withdraw from a race.

EXTRAS – Additional races posted by the Racing Secretary to supplement those in the condition book.

F

FARRIER – A blacksmith.

FETLOCK – The horse's ankle, above the pastern and below the cannon bone.

FIELD – A term for all the horses in a race.

FILLY – A female Thoroughbred that has not reached her fifth birthday or has not been bred.

FLAT RACE – A race contested on level ground rather than a hurdle or steeplechase.

FLATTEN OUT – When a horse drops its head almost on a straight line with its body while running, indicating tiredness.

FLOAT THE TRACK – When the track maintenance crew drags a flat piece of equipment to squeeze the surface water from the racing strip.

FOAL – A baby horse. Also, the process of giving birth. A pregnant mare is referred to as in foal.

FOAL HEAT – The first time a mare comes into season after giving birth, usually after nine days.

FOAL SHARE – An agreement between the owner of a mare and the possessor of a breeding nomination to share the resulting foal either by joint ownership or dividing the proceeds of the sale of that foal. Has many variations.

FOUNDER – The disease laminitis, an inflammation of the horse's hoof caused by changes in blood flow to the foot, overeating, high fever, toxemia, or concussion. Potentially fatal and usually career ending.

FRACTIONAL TIME – Intermediate times in a race registered on the teletimer at the quarter-mile, half, three-quarters, etc.

FULL BROTHER OR SISTER – Horses that have the same sire and dam. A half brother or sister would have the same dam but a different sire.

FURLONG – An eighth of a mile, 220 yards, or 660 feet.

FUROSEMIDE – Also known as Lasix or Salix, a diuretic medication used to treat bleeders, legal in some jurisdictions to be administered pre-race.

FUTURITY – A race for two-year-old horses which have had an entry fee posted before they were born.

G

GALLOP – A fast cantering gait.

GELDING – A castrated male horse.

GET – The offspring of a stallion.

GIRTH and OVERGIRTH – The equipment used to secure the saddle.

GOOD BOTTOM – A track that is firm beneath a sloppy or muddy surface.

GOOD TRACK – The condition of a track between fast and slow as a muddy track dries out.

GRABBING A QUARTER – When the toe of a hind shoe strikes the foreleg on the heel, causing an injury.

GRADED STAKES – The highest quality category of race, assigned I, II or III by the Graded Stakes Committee. Also referred to as Group races outside of North America.

GRANDDAM – The grandmother of a horse.

GRANDSIRE – The grandfather of a horse.

GREEN – A horse who is inexperienced.

GROOM – The employee of a trainer, responsible for the daily care of a horse. May take care of three or more horses.

H

HALTER – Headgear similar to a bridle but lacking a bit. Used to handle horses in the stable when they are not being ridden.

HALTERMAN – Slang for a trainer who claims horses on a regular basis.

HAND – The unit measuring the height of horses at the withers, equaling four inches.

HAND RIDE or HANDILY – When the rider urges his horse without using his whip.

HANDICAP – A race in which the weight carried by the horses is determined by the Racing Secretary, based on their prior performance, and intended to give them all a chance to win.

HARD BOOT – A Kentucky horseman.

HEALTH CERTIFICATE – The standard form concerning a horse's health, required for interstate or international travel.

HIP NUMBER – The number assigned to a horse at auction; their number in the catalog.

HOCK – The part of a horse's rear leg between the gaskin and the cannon.

HOOF DRESSING – A salve or paste used to keep the horse's foot from becoming brittle or cracking.

HORSE – A male equine, five years of age or older, not gelded.

HOTWALKER – A person or mechanical device used to lead a horse to cool it down after exercise.

HUNG – A horse tiring but holding their position in a race, unable or unwilling to pass another.

I

IDENTIFIER – The person tasked with examining all horses before a race by checking the lip tattoo and matching the horse with the description on their foal certificate.

IN FOAL – A pregnant mare.

INQUIRY – A Stewards' investigation into the running of a race when there is a possibility of an infraction.

J

JOCKEY CLUB REGISTRATION CERTIFICATE – A document assigned to each foal that includes their physical description, registration number, and race record. Required to buy or sell a horse.

L

LAMINITIS – See FOUNDER.

LASIX – See FUROSEMIDE.

LAY-UP – A horse sent from the track to a farm to recover from an injury or illness, or just for a rest.

LEAD PONY – A horse used to accompany a racehorse to the post.

LENGTH – The measure of a horse from nose to tail, approximately eight feet, used to determine the distance between horses in a race. In terms of time, commonly considered equal to one-fifth of a second.

M

MAIDEN – A racehorse that has never won a race. Also, a female horse that has never been bred.

MARE – A female horse five years old or older, or younger if she has been bred.

MUDDER – A horse that runs best on a wet track.

MUZZLE – The nose and lips of a horse. Also, a device placed over the horse's mouth to prevent biting or eating in period of time before a race.

N

NEAR SIDE – The left side of the horse, from which they are mounted or led.

NECK – Approximately one-quarter length.

NOM-DE-COURSE – Assumed name of an owner, stable, or partnership.

NON-SWEATER – A horse unable to perspire normally.

O

OAKS – A stakes race for three-year-old fillies.

OBJECTION - A claim of foul lodged by one rider against another.

ODDS-ON – Less than even money.

OFF SIDE – The right side of a horse.

ON THE BIT – A horse eager to run.

OSSLET – A calcium deposit in the fetlock joint which impedes movement.

OVERWEIGHT – A jockey coming in at a weight in excess of the assigned amount for a horse in a race. Limited to five pounds.

OWNERSHIP REGISTRY – The Jockey Club's registration department, keeping track of ownership of stallions and broodmares.

P

PADDOCK – The area where horses are saddled and paraded before a race.

PALPATION – The physical examination of a mare's ovaries and uterus to determine health and readiness for breeding or the state of a pregnancy.

PARI-MUTUEL – The form of betting at tracks whereby odds are determined by the amount wagered on each horse. Payoffs are calculated after the track and state commissions are deducted.

PATROL JUDGE – A racing official who observes the progress of a race from vantage points around racetrack.

PEDIGREE – The record of a Thoroughbred horse's ancestry, most commonly evaluated through four generations.

PHENYLBUTAZONE – See BUTE.

PLACED – A horse finishing second or third in a race. Stakes-placed would refer to a horse that finished second or third in a stakes event. Some European pedigrees include horses that finish fourth in Group races.

PLATER – Slang for a horse running in claiming races.

PLATES – Short for racing plates, or horse shoes.

POLES – Markers placed around the track indication distances.

POOL – Total money bet on a race, divided by the type of bet.

POST PARADE – The procession of horses going from the paddock to the starting gate "parading" before the spectators.

POST POSITION – Numbered from the rail out, the starting position of each horse in a race.

POST TIME – The time designated for a race to start. Not to be confused with the "off time" when the race actually starts.

PRODUCER – The term for a mare after one of her offspring wins a race.

PUBLIC TRAINER – A trainer whose services are not exclusive to one owner; trains for a daily fee.

PURSE – The money for which horses compete in a race.

Q

QUARTER CRACK – A crack in a horse's hoof wall near the heel on either side, due to a concussion or poor shoeing, or even hereditary. May be debilitating based on its severity.

QUARTER POLE – The marker one-quarter mile from the finish line.

R

RACE DAY MEDICATION – Any medication given on the day a horse is entered to race. Generally prohibited in most jurisdictions with the exception of Lasix in North America.

RACING SECRETARY – The official who drafts conditions for races, writes the condition book, and acts a handicapper assigning weights.

RECEIVING BARN – At some tracks the location in the stable area that accommodates horses shipping in for a race. Also, can refer to a gathering place for horses about to race.

REPOSITORY – The area at an auction sale designated for medical information such as X-rays or endoscopic examinations.

RESERVE – The minimum amount which a consignor will accept for a bid on a horse at public auction.

RNA (Reserve Not Attained) – Used for horses not sold or charged back.

RESTRICTED RACE – A race limited to starters based on their place of breeding or previous purse earnings.

RIDGELING – See CRYPTORCHID.

RUN DOWN – Referring to the abrasion of a horse's heels in a race or workout. Also, refers to the bandages applied to prevent such an injury.

S

SADDLE CLOTH – A cloth worn under the horse's saddle on which their race number is displayed.

SCALE OF WEIGHTS – Fixed imposts to be carried by horses based on their age and gender and adjusted for the time of year and distance.

SCHOOLING – The training practice of making a horse accustomed to the starting gate, paddock, and saddling area.

SELECT SALE – A public auction in which the entrants have been screened with certain criteria, including pedigree and conformation.

SESAMOIDS – The two small bones at the back of the fetlock, held in place by ligaments. A fracture to the sesamoid is usually career ending.

SHADOW ROLL – A band, traditionally made of sheepskin, worn over the horse's nose in order to keep them from seeing shadows on the ground. Similar in nature to blinkers, used to limit the horse's field of vision.

SHEDROW – The aisle outside the stalls in a barn.

SHORT – Referring to a horse that needs more conditioning.

SILKS – See COLORS.

SIRE – The father of a horse.

SIRE PRODUCTION INDEX – Statistical analysis comparing a stallion's offspring from the mares to which he has been bred with the offspring of those same mares when bred to other stallions; a barometer of success for stallions.

SLIPPED – An aborted or resorbed pregnancy.

SOUND – Referring to a horse free being from disease or lameness.

SPIT BOX – The area designated for post-race testing, so named for the days when tests were done by collecting saliva rather than urine or blood. Also called the detention barn or "piss barn."

SPLINT – A hard swelling below the knee or hock indicating a fracture or damage to the splint bones, located on either side of the cannon bone. Usually treatable.

STAKES – The highest class of race in which owners pay a fee to enter and start. Those fees are added to the purse and placing in a stakes will qualify the horse for black type in sales catalogs.

STAKES PRODUCER – A mare with at least one foal that has won or placed in a stakes race.

STALLION – An entire male horse used for breeding.

STALLION SEASON – The right to breed one mare to a particular stallion during a particular breeding season. Also referred to as a nomination.

STALLION SHARE – The undivided fractional ownership interest in a stallion, entitling the owner to breed one mare each year plus an occasional additional breeding. There are usually 40 shares in a syndicate, and each owner is responsible for the expenses of their share.

STANDARD STARTS INDEX (SSI) – Statistical analysis comparing a horse's racing class based on earnings per start per year, calculated and divided into male and female categories. Any horse earning the average for their sex has an SSI of 1.00. A horse with an SSI of 2.0 would have earned twice the average per start of their crop, 0.50, half their crop.

STARTER – The racing official in charge of the starting gate; a horse that runs in a race.

STARTER ALLOWANCE – A race designed to allow claiming horses which have improved their form to run in a non-claiming event. A starter handicap would have weights assigned by the racing secretary.

STAYER – A horse that races in long distance races.

STEWARDS – The three officials tasked with upholding the rules of racing and scrutinizing the running of actual races.

STIFLE – The joint of a horse's rear leg comprised of the femur, tibia, and kneecap.

STRANGLES – A potentially serious and highly contagious equine bacterial infection.

STOOPER – A person who makes money at the track by picking up discarded tickets.

STRETCH – The straightaway section of the racetrack in front of the stands, also known as the homestretch.

STRIDE – A horse's way of moving.

STUD BOOK – The registry and genealogical record of the breed, administrated by The Jockey Club.

STUD FEE – The amount paid for the right to breed a mare to a stallion.

SUCKLING – A young horse that is still nursing from its mother.

SUBSTITUTE RACE – Races published in the condition book for use if one or more of the designated races for that day are not used.

SUITABLE FOR MATING – A mare having two normal ovaries, a normal uterus, and a genital tract.

SWAYBACK – A horse with a dip in their back.

T

TACK – Generally, stable gear. More specifically, the equipment used for training and racing.

TAKE – The commission deducted by a track from the mutuel pools, shared by the track, horsemen, and state.

TEASING – The process of using a male horse to approach a mare in order to determine if she is in heat and amenable to breeding. A male horse or pony called the "teaser" will be used for this process, not the stallion to which the mare will actually be bred.

THOROUGHBRED – The breed of horse used for flat and steeplechase racing; in North America, the breed registered with The Jockey Club or with a similar registry in other countries.

THRUSH – The inflammation of the bottom of a horse's foot. It is a moist, foul-smelling rot and requires treatment.

TONGUE TIE – A strip of cloth or bandage used to tie down a horse's tongue to prevent it from impeding their airway during a race or workout.

TOP LINE – The sire line of a Thoroughbred horse's pedigree. Also, can refer to the profile of a horse's back.

TOTALISATOR – A machine used to create the betting tickets as well as calculate the odds of a race based on the distribution of individual wagers in the betting pools.

TRIPLE CROWN – Term for the classic races for three-year-olds. In the U.S., made up of the Kentucky Derby, Preakness, and Belmont Stakes. In England, the Two Thousand Guineas, the Epsom Derby, and the St. Leger.

TWITCH – A veterinary tool consisting of a stick with a loop of cord at one end, placed around the horse's upper lip and twisted in order to control them for treatment or shoeing.

TWO-MINUTE LICK – The pace in a horse's exercise when they are required to gallop one mile in two minutes.

U

UNDER WRAPS – Term for a horse held in restraint in a race or workout.

UNTRIED – A horse not yet raced or tested for speed in a workout.

V

VALET – The person in the jockeys' room who attends to the riders, maintains their equipment, and assists in saddling.

VETS LIST – A roster of horses which have been observed to have an injury, soreness, or have bled. They must be examined and approved by the track veterinarian before they can race again.

W

WASHY – A horse that breaks out in a sweat before a race.

WEANLING – A suckling taken away from their mother.

WEAVER – A horse that bobs back and forth in their stall as a nervous habit.

WEBBING – The apparatus used at the front of a stall as a barrier in lieu of a door to keep the horse contained.

WIND PUFFS – The soft fluid filling in the rear and above the ankles in the area of the suspensories, usually a result of some strain.

WIND SUCKER – See CRIBBER.

WITHERS – The point at which the neck of the horse meets the shoulders and transitions to the back; where they are measured for height.

WOLF TEETH – The extra teeth located forward from the first upper molar, necessitating removal.

WRONG WAY – The opposite direction from which races are run.

Y

YEARLING – A horse aged between the first New Year's Day after birth and the following January first.

INDEX

A

B

C

F

I

J

M

S

T

U

Y

Z